Fairy Tales and the Female Imagination

Jennifer Waelti-Walters

Eden Press
Montréal Canada

FAIRY TALES & THE FEMALE IMAGINATION
Jennifer Waelti-Walters

268882

© 1982 EDEN PRESS, INC.
Montreal, Quebec, Canada
and
St. Albans, Vermont, U.S.A.

This book has been published with the help of a grant from the Social Science Federation of Canada, using funds provided by the Social Sciences and Humanities Research Council of Canada

ISBN: 0-920792-07-3
First Edition

Printed in Canada by T.H. Best Printing Ltd.

Dépôt légal — deuxième trimestre 1982
Bibliothèque nationale du Québec

All rights reserved. No part of this book may be reproduced, stored in a retrieval system, or transmitted, in any form or by any means, electronic, mechanical, photocopying, recording, or otherwise, without the written permission of Eden Press, Inc.

Grateful acknowledgement is made to the following for permission to quote from: *L'Euguélionne* by Louky Bersianik, Les Editions de la Presse (Montreal); *Les Prunes de Cythère* by Jeanne Hyvrard and *Ce sexe qui n'en est pas un* by Luce Irigaray, Les Editions de Minuit (Paris); *Histoire de la sexualité* by M. Foucault, Les Editions Gallimard (Paris) and Pantheon (New York); *La Jeune née* by Hélène Cixous, Union générale d'éditions (Paris); *The Second Sex* by Simone de Beauvoir and *The Uses of Enchantment* by Bruno Bettelheim and *Madness and Civilization* by M. Foucault, Alfred A. Knopf Inc./Random House (New York); *Gyn/ecology* by Mary Daly, copyright © Mary Daly, reprinted by permission of Beacon Press; *The Divided Self* by R.D. Laing, copyright © Tavistock Publications Ltd.; *Women and Madness* by Phyllis Chesler, Doubleday (New York); *The Manufacture of Madness* by Thomas S. Szasz, Harper and Row (New York); *The Silent Rooms*, by Anne Hébert, General Publishing Co. Ltd. (Toronto); *Les Belles Images* by Simone de Beauvoir, Les Editions Gallimard (Paris); *The Rapture of Lol V. Stein* by M. Duras, Hamish Hamilton Ltd. (London); *Mad Shadows* by Marie-Claire Blais, reprinted by permission, McClelland and Stewart Limited (Toronto); *Les Guérillères* by Monique Wittig, copyright (English language translation) © 1971 by Peter Owen, reprinted by permission of Viking Penguin Inc.; "First Adam then Eve" by James Hillman, Eranos (Switzerland)*; "Une mauvaise lecture" in *Une Mauvaise Lecture* by Constance Delaunay, Editions Gallimard (Paris); *Mooring Buoy/Moored Body* by Monique Bosco, translation by Josée M. LeBlond, Room of One's Own (Vancouver) and Monique Bosco; *Man's World, Woman's Place* © 1972 by Elizabeth Janeway, Delta, reprinted by permission. Permission to reprint is gratefully acknowledged from: University of Louisville for parts of Chapters 3 and 7; *International Journal of Women's Studies* for most of Chapter 1; *The Journal of Canadian Fiction* for Chapter 4; *The New York Literary Forum* for part of Chapter 7.

*This has been published subsequently in *The Myth of Analysis*, Harper Colophon, 1978.

*For my mother, Aunt Barbara, Elizabeth and Pam,
in memory of Grandma.*

*For my fighting friends: Janet, Laura, Viviane,
Pat, Pauline and Paddy.*

*And to the next generation: Leila, Alissa, Ruth and Maia,
Lise, Bronwen, Amy and Fiona.*

BY THE AUTHOR

Alchimie et littérature, à propos de *Portrait de l'artiste en jeune singe,* Paris, Denoel, Collection Dossiers des Lettres Nouvelles, 1975.

Michel Butor, Victoria, B.C., Sono Nis Press, 1977.

J.M.G. Le Clézio, Boston, Twayne World Author Series, 1977.

Icare ou l'évasion impossible: étude psycho-mythique de l'oeuvre de J.M.G. Le Clézio, Sherbrooke, Éditions Naaman, 1981.

CONTENTS

PART I: MIRROR, MIRROR ON THE WALL

Chapter 1
    On princesses: fairy tales, sex roles and loss of self. 1
Chapter 2
    Beauty and the Beast and *The Silent Rooms* (Hébert). 13
Chapter 3
    Snow White and *Les Belles Images* (Beauvoir). 31
Chapter 4
    Cinderella and *Mad Shadows* (Blais) 45
Chapter 5
    Sleeping Beauty and *The Rapture of Lol V. Stein* (Duras). 58

PART II: THE MIRROR CRACKED FROM SIDE TO SIDE

Chapter 6
    On witches: power, sexuality and language. 77
Chapter 7
    And the flesh was made word: *The Prunes of Cythera*
    (Hyvrard) and *Les Guérillères* (Wittig). 92
Chapter 8
    And dwelt among us: *The Eugélionne* (Bersianik) 113
Chapter 9
    A fairy tale conclusion: "A bad reading" (Delaunay). 134

Notes 146
An Idiosyncratic Bibliography 156
Index 159

Fairy Tales and the Female Imagination

···∘Part I···

And there she wove by night and day
A magic web with colours gay
For she had heard a whisper say
A curse is on her if she stay
       To look down to Camelot.
She knows not what that curse may be
And so she weaveth steadily
And little other care has she
       The Lady of Shalott.

***

She left the web, she left the loom
She took three paces through the room
She saw the helmet and the plume
       And she looked down to Camelot
Out flew the web and floated wide
The mirror cracked from side to side
The curse has come upon me cried
       The Lady of Shalott.

                            Tennyson

CHAPTER 1

ON PRINCESSES:
FAIRY TALES, SEX ROLES AND LOSS OF SELF[1]

Nobody in her right mind could possibly want to be a fairy tale princess. After all, what do they do except play dead across the path of some young man who has been led to believe that he rules the world? In every really famous tale the heroine is systematically deprived of affection, stimulation, pleasurable activity, instruction and even companionship. She is a totally powerless prisoner, in turn the victim of circumstance, of an older woman and of men of all ages. Yet every one of us has been tricked into believing that she would like to be just that at some time in her life. Conclusion: at that moment she was not in her right mind.

Why then are these stories told so assiduously to little girls? Because they sum up perfectly the situation of women in modern western society both in their content and in the telling of them; the pill is sugared, administered and produces change. The message given by the stories and implicit in all social exchanges, against which women are now struggling, was laid out very clearly in Simone de Beauvoir's seminal analysis *The Second Sex*[2] : woman is made not born ("On ne naît pas femme, on la devient.") The crucial point then becomes "Who makes her?" Until now, in our society, there has been an unquestioned male response: "We do of course" — answer which can also be found in Beauvoir's work: " 'From now on I will take you in hand,' Sartre said when he announced my success in the aggregation to me."[3] That Beauvoir, an informed, intelligent feminist, should be able to write this without comment in 1958, nine years after the publication of *The Second Sex*, proves more clearly than any other example I have ever seen the insidiousness of the formation women undergo. The reading of fairy tales is one of the first steps in the maintenance of a misogynous, sex-role stereotyped patriarchy, for what is the end product

1

of these stories by a lifeless humanoid, malleable, decorative, and interchangeable — that is, a "feminine woman" who is inherited, bartered or collected in a monstrous game of Monopoly.

In a partiarchial society such as ours, woman is kept apart from all positions of power, all policy making, all situations in which she might pose a threat to the phallocratic *status quo*, in the most logical and efficient way possible: she is kept apart from herself. Deprived of a developed sense of identity, deprived therefore of self-esteem, she is forced to accept as hers the value other people put upon her; as I said, an object in a commercial system of exchange. Bettelheim lays out the situation and the way in which fairy tales perpetuate it (albeit unbeknown to himself) in *The Uses of Enchantment*[4].

> The parent in such fairy tales, far from resenting the child's transcending his oedipal attachment to him, is delighted he has and often is instrumental in arranging it. For example, in "Hans, My Hedgehog" and in "Beauty and the Beast" the father (willingly or unwillingly) causes his daughter to marry; relinquishing his oedipal attachment to his daughter and inducing her to give up hers to him lead to a happy solution for both.
>
> Never in a fairy tale does a son take his father's kingdom away from him. If a father gives it up, it is always because of old age. Even then the son has to earn it, by finding the most desirable woman for himself, as in "The Three Feathers." This story makes it quite clear that gaining the kingdom is tantamount to having reached moral and sexual maturity. First one task . . . The third task is to find and bring home the right bride; when the hero manages to do this, the kingdom is finally his. Thus, far from projecting the son's being jealous of his father, or the father's resenting his son's sexual endeavors, the fairy story tells the opposite: when the child has reached the right age and maturity, the parent wants him to come into his own sexually also; in fact he will accept his son as a worthy successor only after he has done so.
>
> In many fairy stories a king gives his daughter in marriage to the hero and either shares his kingdom with him or installs him as the eventual successor. This is, of course, a wishful fantasy of the child. But since the story assures him that this is indeed what is going to happen, and since in the unconscious the "king" stands for one's own father, the fairy tale promises the highest possible reward — a happy life and the kingdom — to the son who through

his struggles has found the right solution to his oedipal conflicts: to transfer his love for his mother to a suitable partner of his own age; and to recognize that the father (far from being a threatening competitor) is really a benevolent protector who approves of his son's finding adult fulfillment.

Gaining his kingdom through being united in love and marriage with the most appropriate and desirable partner — a union which the parents fully approve and which leads to happiness for everybody but the villains — symbolizes the perfect resolution of oedipal difficulties, as well as the gaining of true independence and complete personality integration. Is it really all that unrealistic to speak of such high achievement as coming into one's own kingdom? (pp. 129-130)

For a girl too? In the first paragraph the daughter is *"caused* to marry." In the second she is the "most desirable woman" the prince can find, the prince's task being "to find and bring home the right bride". In the third paragraph "a king *gives* his daughter in marriage to the hero and either shares his kingdom with *him* or installs *him* as eventual successor." "This is, of course, a wishful fantasy of the child" Bettelheim goes on to say; which child? Can Bettelheim really believe his own brief protest that fairy tales play no role in sexual stereotyping (p. 226) and maintain honestly that a girl child can withstand being handed from man to man as a possession, albeit a precious one, and still keep the fantasy that she is the hero and will gain her kingdom in the sense of "gaining a feeling of selfhood and of self-worth and a sense of moral obligation" (p. 6) required by Bettelheim? She will inevitably reach sexual maturity with time, but her moral maturity would seem to be limited to an acceptance of selflessness — selflessness: a nice Christian, virtuous name for objecthood. It this not sexual stereotyping?

If we look at a well-known story in detail we shall see that it is indeed. "Snow White" is an overt commercial for marriage, carrying within it the message that all that matters in a woman is her appearance. It is preferable that in all other aspects she be dead. The prince chooses the girl in the coffin — a picture in a frame — and it is only by accident that the apple is jolted out of her throat. Death and marriage go hand in hand.

The first queen died giving birth to her daughter and the new queen is there to kill Snow White as soon as she is of age to challenge her mother's supremacy in the only realm in which she has ever been rewarded: the beauty contest. Mother is divided into three roles all working to one end. First there is the model to which the girl aspires: she is the "real" mother and she is dead. Next is the teacher, seen by the child as a persecutor: the wicked step-mother, who has a mirror image in the helper: the fairy godmother or good old woman who tells the girl how to win the prince. One and all reduce her independence, undermine her self-esteem and sense of identity and drain her vitality; they offer in exchange the image of a beautiful doll (herself) which she can play with in a mirror until it begins to wear out and, like all dolls, she is replaced.

In her book *Gyn/Ecology*[5] Mary Daly reinforces my argument for she writes:

> Patriarchy perpetuates its deception through myth. Before considering specific myths or conglomerates of them, it is important to look briefly at language about them. On the banal level of everyday cliché, one often hears, "It's only a myth (or story, or fairy tale, or legend)." The cliché belittles the power of myth. The child who is fed tales such as *Snow White* is not told that the tale itself is a poisonous apple, and the Wicked Queen (her mother/teacher), having herself been drugged by the same deadly diet throughout her lifetime (death-time), is unaware of her venomous part in the patriarchal plot. (p. 44)

She then goes on to criticise the deliberately confusing language used in patriarchal interpretations of myth and fairy tale by other scholars as "reputable" as Bettelheim.

Women are divided against each other in a thankless struggle to gain a master, displaying, as a group, an excellent example of slave mentality. Divided they remain fallen and nobody seems to care. The queen probably does not dislike her destructive role because it helps her turn into an acceptable channel the rage she feels as she watches her daughter daily becoming more beautiful while she herself fades. But as long as the king lives she will be queen. She holds the position in thrall from her husband and Snow White is not therefore a direct challenger for her throne. The girl must be provided with the necessary attributes to get one of her own. Dependency is the only future offered: marriage to a man who will govern her, who needs a mother for his heirs (and for himself) and an ornament for his home; something useful, delightful to look at and no trouble; an object with no selfhood and no autonomy — a dead thing who will kill in her turn.

Thus the initiation of the mothers is visited on the daughters of the third and fourth generation. Man's description of the way he desires woman to be in order to maintain his *status quo* has been so well established — women having been denied access until recently to the instruction which would enable them to create their own description of themselves — knowledge about women having been so thoroughly transferred into the realm of male authority, that the women have come to see themselves as perfect secretaries one and all, whose role in life is to administer ruthlessly the whims and world view of their bosses. This too is incorporated into the description of woman's place provided by the best known fairy tales. The mirror into which we all look turns back a cracked image labelled "desirable."

From birth a little girl is required to respond constantly to demands from outside that she should fit into a certain pattern. She must be pretty, well-dressed, quiet, well-behaved: in two words decoratively unobtrusive. She matches up to the ideal to the best of her ability because she is afraid she will not be loved if she does not — and how right she is to fear! — but if she is ugly, active, intelligent, talkative, the strain of meeting impossible criteria is such that the inner self finally revolts. The result of this refusal of the imposed values frequently takes the form of madness or a state verging on insanity — a "nervous breakdown," a "depression" — a violent crisis which is the only way she can take action and thus shatter the unsustainable role.

Social demands push women into schizophrenic behaviours (as described by R.D. Laing[6]), dividing them within themselves, mutilating them by creating a restrictive environment within which they cannot live. Some are driven crazy and many others, who do not succumb to the initiation into madness, are arbitrarily labelled insane by those who want to punish them for their resistance, i.e. insubordination.[7]

Time and again in fairy tales boys are sent off on adventures for seven years or so. What do girls do in similar circumstances? They are repressed: they must not speak or laugh; they must sit in a tree and sew or undego some similar initiation into martyrdom. Girls have their hands cut off, are sent to live with monsters, all to save their father from death until their brothers or husband arrive back to inherit the kingdom. In short, they are taught to be passive victims.

This deliberate mutilation is expressed even more openly in Hans Andersen's writings than in the tales of the Brothers Grimm.[8] That it is a curtailment of liberty as ferocious as that of foot binding in China[9] is inescapable. All Andersen's major heroines are imprisoned, lamed or have no shoes: the little mermaid, the dancer in the "Tin Soldier," the little matchgirl, Karen in "The Red Shoes." In the Grimm tales the recurrent symbol is rather that of a girl being imprisoned or forced to wear a mask or obliged to play dead: she is separated from her true self. Bettelheim is perhaps right when he postulates that at one level these symbols provide an encouragement to some children that they will eventually escape their situation of being in the power of adults: incitements to patience and hope. But other children, namely most girls, never escape this original situation; for them the tales provide a symbolic description of a set of symptoms which are distressingly like the depiction of the split self of a schizoid personality as defined by Laing:

> The term schizoid refers to an individual the totality of whose experience is split in two main ways: in the first place, there is a rent in his relation with his world and, in the second, there is a disruption of his relation with himself. Such a person is not able to experience himself "together with" others or "at home in" the world, but, on the contrary, he experiences himself in despairing aloneness and isolation; moreover, he does not experience himself as a complete persone but rather as "split" in various ways, perhaps as a mind more or less tenuously linked to a body, as two or more selves, and so on. (p. 17)

→ The prince in fairy tales is always together with others. His quest is to establish himself amongst his peers and be rewarded for it. The princess is relegated to the kitchen, shut in a tower, exiled, killed and no matter how hard she works to fulfill the tasks given, her taskmaster or mistress is never satisfied. Yet despite such blatant differences in treatment in all the stories he discusses, Bettelheim assimilates girls with boys by implication and omission throughout his book. He begins commendably thus:

> Today, as in times past, the most important and also the most difficult task in raising a child is helping him to find meaning in life. Many growth experiences are needed to achieve this. The child, as he develops, must learn step by step to understand himself better; with this he becomes more able to understand others, and eventually can relate to them in ways which are mutually satisfying and meaningful.
>
> To find deeper meaning, one must become able to transcend the narrow confines of a self-centered existence and believe that one will make a significant contribution to life — if not right now, then at some future time. This feeling is necessary if a person is to be satisfied with himself and with what he is doing. In order not to be at the mercy of the vagaries of life, one must develop one's

inner resources, so that one's emotions, imagination, and intellect mutually support and enrich one another. Our positive feelings give us the strength to develop our rationality; only hope for the future can sustain us in the adversities we unavoidably encounter. (pp. 3-4)

All very fine and good; dutiful parents can nod sagely in agreement with this authoritative, avuncular figure who continues:

> It is here that fairy tales have unequalled value, because they offer new dimensions to the child's imagination which would be impossible for him to discover as truly on his own. Even more important, the form and structure of fairy tales suggest images to the child by which he can structure his daydreams and with them give better direction to his life. (p. 7)

How many people reconsider the truth of these statements in the context of the male orientation of the rest of the book?

How many people realize that fairy tales provide girls with none of these desirable steps? The weight of professional discourse puts blinkers on us once again.

It is my contention that fairy tales — "Cinderella," "Snow White," "Sleeping Beauty," and "Beauty and the Beast" in particular, being the ones which are best known today — do not help little girls to achieve autonomy in the way they help boys. On the contrary they hold girls back. They offer only one security: that of being loved by father or his substitute.[10] This is a deliberate prolongation of the oedipal stage with its implied substructure of dependency and physical dissatisfaction/sexual immaturity. Hence it is a negation of the ontological security necessary for a child to achieve autonomy and, I quote Laing once more:

> A firm sense of one's own autonomous identity is required in order that one may be related as one human being to another. Otherwise, any and every relationship threatens the individual with loss of identity. (p. 44)

Fairy tales teach girls to accept at least a partial loss of identity, and thus endanger all the relationships in which they must take part in a lifetime. These relationships are further jeopardized by the fact that the same tales transmit to boys an overt possessor/object, master/slave relationship pattern, the playing out of which will reinforce the self-destructive, victim pattern of behaviour taught to girls.

Jungian analysis, as presented in the extensive writings of Marie-Louise von Franz,[11] does nothing to re-establish the balance, as she interprets the stories as archetypal aspects of the ego, the self and the anima. Girls are thereby absorbed into the old traditional patterns of mother goddess, or Koré, or into man as his "feminine side."

To explain my divergence from the theories of Bettelheim and von Franz let me borrow Laing's words once more:

> [Woman] can be seen as person or thing. Now, even the same thing, seen from different points of view, gives rise to two entirely different descriptions, and the descriptions give rise to two entirely different theories, and the theories result in two entirely different sets of action. The initial way we see a thing determines all our subsequent dealings with it. (p. 20)

Fairy tales present girls as objects; they are perceived as objects thereafter by everyone (girl and boy alike) who is not provided with an equally powerful counter-description. Until very recently such a description of woman by women has not been attempted. Both fairy tales and psychology are part of an accepted, male oriented view of the world which has become second nature to us all and which has been the unchallenged "ghost in the machine" in all scientific and philosophical work for centuries. One of the best descriptions I have found of the situation is given by James Hillman in his long essay "First Adam, then Eve."[12] After tracing the Western outlook from Aristotle and Genesis through to Freud, he says:

> The image of female inferiority has not changed because it remains the image in the masculine psyche. Theories of the female body are preponderantly based on the observations and fantasies of men. These theories are statements of masculine consciousness confronted with its sexual opposite. We must bear in mind that the evidence in anatomy, as in all fields of science, is gathered mainly by men and is part of their philosophy. (p. 374)

He goes on to comment on the way men have formed the way we look at things and the way we treat them, and continues:

> We have called this consciousness Apollonic for, like its namesake it belongs to youth, it kills from a distance (its distance

kills), it never merges with nor "marries" its material, keeping the scientific cult of objectivity. It is a structure of consciousness that has an estranged relation with the feminine which we have taken to mean "the abysmal side of bodily man with his animal passions and instinctual nature, and 'matter' in general" . . . This structure produces these theories of the human body as part of a philosophy which guarantees the superiority of male consciousness and the inferiority of whatever opposite with which it will be conjoined. And there is no way out of the dilemma as long as this Jahvistic or Apollonic structure informs not only scientific thought but *the very nature of consciousness itself* [his italics] . . . For this kind of consciousness, the elevation of the female principle seems structurally impossible; it is driven to repeat the same misogynist views century after century because of its archetypal base. (p. 375)

This misogynous base is now being challenged, but against great odds, odds which must be measured by the implication of Laing's statement that: "sanity or psychosis is tested by the degree of conjunction or disjunction between two persons where one is sane by common consent" (p. 36) against Hillman's description of a male controlled consensus: men who conform to social norms — including the repression of women — are thereby necessarily sane. All who protest — especially women — are mad.[13] By this reasoning women are either acceptably insane: passive and schizoid, or unacceptably insane: active and autonomous. This latter condition is, for men, normal, acceptable sanity.

In such a double bind, it is one thing to recognize, once adult, that the structures and traditions of society push you along a path leading to chronic frustration and insecurity, it is quite another to resist them. It is even more difficult to help a child to circumvent the obstacles in her path to a healthy development as a fully functioning human being. Women are under a constant threat of being labelled mad — a crank, a hysteric, menopausal or unreasonable, all versions of the same — and thereupon losing what little attention is now paid to them, what little value they have left. Madness is held over them as a punishment which comes of itself to those who accept their role against their will and which is imposed by men on most of those who dare refuse it. It is not even sufficient to take the pittance that society offers; you must actually accept it into youself and become the image demanded if you are not to suffer a fate worse than death, for "death" is the fate you have anyway.

Half-life: madness or atrophy. Witch and princess, hag and virgin are the two images constantly projected onto women by long centuries of theological, philosophical and literary tradition. Both roles must be exorcized before a woman can take her place in the world and describe herself in an authoritative discourse. Both are man-declared pariahs, excluded from the arena of human (i.e. male) activity and forced to live in a state of mind-body schism.

The desirability of the powerless role and terror of the sanctions imposed on female knowledge are traps out of which every woman must climb before she can achieve autonomy and a secure sense of herself. She cannot however do this in isolation. She is a part of a group whose dynamics continue to act upon her, reinforcing her long-conditioned responses. A princess needs a king, queen and prince to prove her title, and all act together as a schizophrenogenic family keeping each other captive in their game of domination and subservience.[14]

The novels discussed in this volume offer case studies of women aware of this mask clamped over their living faces and who are struggling to come to terms with their situation, their inner division and the ever-present threat of madness: real or labelled. In Anne Hébert's *The Silent Rooms* (1958) Catherine's husband imprisons her and limits her life in a deliberate attempt to "purify" her. Not until she is on the verge of death does she turn and fight for her right to exist. Laurence, heroine of Simone de Beauvoir's *Les Belles Images* (1958) rejects in a more reasoned but no less painful revolt the image imposed upon her by her mother and husband, and which she was about to transfer to her daughter. Laurence breaks the chain of mirror-image mother/daughter situations, but Isabelle-Marie, in Marie-Clarie Blais' *Mad Shadows* (1959), continues it, despite her awareness of the results for Anne. *Les Belles Images* and *Mad Shadows* are two faces of the same coin: a family network where in the one case the roles can be modified and in the other everyone is locked into a destructive spiral of violence and self-destruction. Marguerite Duras, in the *Rapture of Lol V. Stein* (1964), recounts the history of a woman's identity split and the subsequent long, slow reintegration of her mind and body.

Hébert, Beauvoir, Blais and Duras all portray heroines trying to come to terms with the behaviour society requires of them, or to reject the imposed image in favour of a new and more accurate description of themselves. What more natural then, than that one of the earliest pictures of their role given to little girls — that of the fairy tale princess — should be incorporated into their reassessment? Catherine is Beauty ("Beauty and the Beast"); Laurence, Snow White; Isabelle-Marie, Cinderella; Lol Stein, Sleeping Beauty.

This substructure, picked up (and perhaps also written in) subconsciously, resonates deep in the basic role formation of each reader and causes a violent reaction to the novel. The description on both levels is that of a split being whose inner self is separated from the outer appearance of self, playing the necessary social role, and who feels guilt and failure in the face of the separation. Rejection of the given role, awareness of self, come together in a fear of being considered hysterical or mad; fear which must be overcome before the label can be rejected and an integrated being with the courage to enunciate her own values can emerge from between mad Scylla and virgin Charbidys.

The movement of these fears, rejections, identifications, desires, guilt, which shift between the conscious and unconscious mind of the heroine, have their mirror image in the split-level discourse of the novels. Every woman has been to some extent conditioned by "Cinderella," "Snow White" *et al*, and her reaction to them creates a complex series of reflections back and forth between the text, the subtext (fairy tale) as it exists in the novel and also as it is stirred up in her mind, thus expressing her anxieties and perhaps ambivalence as she sees her role being redefined as she reads. The pressures are multiple and many are far too subtle to be controlled.

The structure of the novels themselves duplicates this pattern of the pressures of tradition in the way in which the half perceived fairy tale, lying beneath the revolt in the text, pulls constantly against it, conjuring (in my mind at least), against everything the heroine feels and the view we are given of her impossible situation, a vague recurrent belief that it will all work out and they will live happily ever after. A belief which, in the circumstances, is undesirable, unjustifiable rubbish. The old magic, the quiet conditioning is very strong — after all, a woman is created to serve man in marriage, no? All the (male) authorities on record since Aristotle wrote *On the generation of animals* have agreed that her contribution is inferior[15] and that is what we have all been taught; hence the guilt and fear of being insane expressed by the women who refuse this second-rate humanity adjudged their lot and the nagging of the fairy tale beneath each one's experience.

To be acceptable a woman has always had to try and fit the tale. What is demanded of a princess? That she be good, beautiful and long-suffering; that she put up with every misery those around impose upon her. And why? Because then, one day a prince will come and marry her. In short, that she fulfill to the letter the requirements of education summed up by August Comte in the nineteenth century, in his *Système de politique positive:*[16]

> It is in order to better develop her moral superiority that woman must gratefully accept the rightful practical domination of man . . . First as a mother, and soon as a sister, then above all as a wife, and finally as a daughter, marginally as a maid-servant, in these four natural roles woman is destined to preserve man from

the corruption inherent in his practical and theoretical existence. Her emotional superiority directly gives her this fundamental duty, which social economy develops increasingly by releasing the loving sex from all disturbing cares, active or speculative.

He has the dubious grace to offer moral superiority as a sop to his female slave; even this has disappeared from the succinct directive to be found in an *Encyclopédie de la femme* published in Paris in 1950.[17] Under the rubric "Women's education" we find:

> She must make herself, in the most altruistic sense. The role of woman in life is to give to all around her: comfort, joy, beauty, while maintaining a smile, without appearing to be a martyr, with no bad temper, with no visible fatigue. It is a heavy task. Our daughter must be trained into this perpetual and happy renunciation. From the first year of her life, she must know how to share spontaneously her toys, her candy, and give away what she has, *especially* what she cares for most.

Girls have been taught for centuries that they should commit a smiling, lifelong suicide, deny their own nature, have no identity whatsoever.

The struggle to refuse all such training, models and approval, to take responsibility for your own life and step resolutely out of the prison of a prolonged childhood into a hostile environment in which you have no guaranteed place is a hard one indeed, but one which gives fresh significance to the quotation I used early in this chapter: "On ne nait pas femme, on la devient"; you are not born a woman, you become one. It is the transfer from "being made" to "becoming" that is difficult.

CHAPTER 2

"BEAUTY AND THE BEAST"
AND *THE SILENT ROOMS* (Hébert)

Little girls who read too many fairy stories believe in princes with long, delicate hands and fine aristocratic features, who will take them away from the drudgery of their daily lives to fine castles where they will be entertained and waited on. They sit and dream and wait: some day my prince will come and we shall live happily ever after. Until they find themselves inside the story for ever after, they never consider the implications of the sequence of events. Once the prince arrives there is no escaping him whether life in the palace is pleasant or not — but it should all work out in the end. There is even a story for such circumstances: it is called "Beauty and the Beast" and that is the one Catherine gets caught in.

All the necessary elements of a fairy story are present in *The Silent Rooms*[1] as we shall see: there is a poor girl and a prince in disguise, a dying father and a stepmother, a castle deep in the forest. We shall find the atmosphere of the early part of "Beauty and the Beast" and even some of the circumstancial details as we remember them from our childhood. All of which adds power to Anne Hébert's novel by giving it a level of unexpected and largely subconscious resonance for the reader. This is why Catherine's situation is extremely painful to us: we all expect the usual, implacable march towards happiness, even though we see that our expectation is at odds with the actual words of the text, for Catherine herself never considers Michel without a specifically stated degree of anxiety. The fairy tale substructure works constantly against the manifest presentation of a modern trauma, and that substructure is blocked before its natural resolution, creating a tension which prevents the apparent solution to Catherine's troubles from ringing true. A profound dissatisfaction reigns despite the sunshine of the last section of the novel.

This indispensible dissatisfaction is what gives *The Silent Rooms* its bite, because it is the very malaise that is felt by a large number of women today, and it is produced in the same way. We all have deeply rooted subconscious expectations, into which we have been conditioned, which prevent us from seeing our situation clearly even when we look at it with our eyes wide open. Catherine knows she will be unhappy living with Michel but she does not believe it because he is the local prince-equivalent, ("le fils du Seigneur"). Certainly she is trapped by her family situation and the expectations held for girls, but she it is who selects Michel, who is mesmerized by the "barbarian prince" rather than settling for some more ordinary neighbour. The novel has a lot to teach us about the way women are taught to be victims and to believe they are princesses. Let us look at it more closely.

Motherless, Catherine is pushed into marriage by her aunt (temporary stepmother) to save her father who is losing his strength (dying) and must find husbands for his daughters. Therefore, she, the eldest, goes to the rich and frightening creature in the foreboding castle in the woods who is known to live a mysterious life of secret anguish and excess. Beauty stays with the Beast from pity; he gives her beautiful clothes, a splendid bed, jewels, but keeps her prisoner. She is not allowed to do anything, not allowed out and sees the Beast for only one hour in the evening, when he is kind and attentive. If she tries to see him at any other time he treats her very badly. She realizes he suffers torment all night long and sleeps all day. Beauty tries to meet the Beast's requirements and help him, but she thinks of her little sisters and is distressed. The Beast promises to let her return home, but she only manages to leave when she has fallen ill from loneliness and is about to die. Once she returns home she rediscovers her health, her joy in life and in her family. She has returned from the dead, but the Beast's suffering is on her conscience.

The Silent Rooms ends here. However, we are not free of our knowledge that she will return to him — disquieting knowledge in this instance because right from the beginning this tale is full of complex, equivocal emotions and a very strong sense of Catherine as victim (a knowing and masochistically willing victim). There is none of the usual reassurance that this Beast has a heart of gold or indeed any heart at all under his egocentric anguish. Catherine seems to be held by pity and a desperate need to be a princess no matter how uncomfortable it may be. (And it is uncomfortable: Lia speaks of "infinite leisure and wild anguish"; the story of the super-sensitive princess and the pea is mentioned also.) After all, princesses are loved and live happily, don't they?

Catherine is not mature. Her mother's death deprived her of her childhood too soon, but she has not achieved adulthood. Time and again she is called adolescent and her physical appearance is that of a child. When she should be looking practically at the men around her in order to get a husband, she deliberately maintains the double state necessary to find a prince: that of childhood — to believe in him, and that of being hardworking, because in stories the good, hardworking, long-suffering girls are always discovered and carried off:

> The men of the region were rough and wild, and the pale girl with her too short skirts and bony knees would pretend to be working or affect a childish air whenever one of them stopped to look at her and wish her good evening. She wanted to nurture her dream and remain aloof, as defiant and mysterious as a woman secretly in pursuit of a barbarian prince. (p. 11)

Indeed, she has already seen and recognised her prince in the feverish little boy who followed his huntsman father out of the fog one day when she was lost; he appealed to her pity. The father, distant and taciturn, resembled her own, and the children's situations were parallel in that she also carried a heavy weight imposed by her father. This was the year of her mother's death and so from the start the relationship is complicated by symbolic overtones. The appearance of a sort of alter ego out of the fog marked Catherine. She stored it away in her heart "along with other sombre and sacred objects — such as the death of her mother, and her own interrupted childhood" (p. 8), and it resurfaced immediately in a dream in which the likeness is manifest — the little boy and his grief are inseparable and apart from the world; an image of Catherine herself:

> On the top shelf of the cupboard among orderly piles of linen, the seigniorial manor lay in the hollow of a glass ball, like a ship in a bottle. The perfume of trees was captured there and the endless misery of a little boy, bereft of all compassion. When Catherine seized the glass ball in her hands, rain and fog fell, slowly upon the manor, the trees and the child's misery. As if an hourglass had been inverted, the entire image was washed away. (p. 8)

The dream reflects the same gloom and suffering, fog and rain as the first meeting, as well as the distance separating Catherine and Michel — distance which transforms itself into time. By this omen, Catherine's sense of being linked inevitably to Michel and of being unable to see clearly where she is going, or reach and alleviate the suffering that is the essence of the boy, are established and will develop throughout the first part of *The Silent Rooms*.

However it is also a picture of Catherine locked into her unexpressed grief, a fragile child full of emotions for which there are no outlet, and which only time will drain away. Beauty is drawn to the Beast by the anguish they seem to share, but which separates them like the wall of glass. It is no wonder that mist, rain and shadows mark their encounter.

When Michel does not come to meet her at the concert:

> A land of mist and forest rose before her. Once again she was meeting an arrogant seigneur in hunting boots and a dark girl, as prickly as a cactus, and then the image of a terrified little boy came into focus and took on the shape of a man. (p. 15)

When he does come, they meet at the edge of the forest in which it is already dark. When she refuses to meet him, she closes the house up tightly "using as a pretext the fog and that earthy smell that pervaded the town with the descent of the long autumn evenings" (p. 36), and her father spends a contented evening also, protected from his bereavement.

The atmosphere is that of gothic stories and the black side of fairy tales, mysterious, threatening, and it gathers thickest around Michel's home. Catherine does not find it reassuring, yet it fascinates her and she can not take her eyes off it, thinking of the women who have lived there. She swears never to return to it herself however, and:

> She swore never to see Michel again, steeling herself as if afraid of being turned into a statue of salt at the least sign of regret. (p. 37)

A statue of salt — death from tears. Catherine is frightened of her lot as a victim of the stepmother-witch figures she evokes yet she dare not slacken her self-control because the force of the pent-up suffering inside her would kill her. Even in her most desperate moment of crisis she plays dead. She suffers and is under a spell but still she will not cry.

Her control makes her appear dead, but it is this very control which is her last remaining instinct for self-preservation. Her suffering is all she has left of herself and Michel wants even that. He wants to drown her, and almost manages to do it:

> She grew limp, languid, exhausted, without strength; she was about to dissolve into a flood of tears when the voice of her delirium soared again, clear and precise, rising from the bottom of her alerted heart: "This woman is so beautiful that I'd like to drown her."

> She gave a piercing shriek . . . She pushed him away, hitting him squarely in the chest with both hands . . . Michel's lost love suddenly welled up anew in her heart. She was struggling for her life against the strange love of this man. (p. 117)

Michel himself is as if drowned after he has made love to Catherine and complains about "this decaying love" ("cet amour pourri").

They are caught in a nightmarish spiral of mutual inhibition and mutual need which spins back into childhood. For Michel, childhood is the enchanted state to which he wishes to return; he seems to believe that if he can turn Catherine into the image of his dead mother the spell of his anguish will be broken and as in the fairy tale, "I'll reclaim the house . . . We'll cross the threshold together with your hand on my arm, like the true lords and masters of the place" (p. 102).

To struggle against such a demand is difficult for Catherine because she has already played her own mother's role for her sisters, and she has not articulated her need to be loved as a woman in her own right, so she still responds to the idealised picture of the fairy tale princess as the archetypal victim. Lia recognises the danger she represents however, her potential power to destroy what remains of Michel's early life by forcing him to grow up, and denounces Catherine to Michel (p. 116).

After all, she, Lia, began the destruction when she took a lover and Michel continued it by his marriage. As Lia says, "it's only fair that our childhood home should be taken from us. Didn't we betray it, both of us?" (p. 102). The betrayal lies in the act of growing up. Adulthood is associated with death for all three, so they are afraid to take the final step and accept their transformation; hence the pull of the house, the constant desire to return to the manor house ("la maison des seigneurs"). But it holds the shadows of adolescence, the passions and pains that must come out into the light.

Catherine's little sisters are quite sure that it is an undesirable place (and the idea of the wicked witch in the woods is not far away — especially when we remember the description given by their uncle of a woman with an owl's face who lived there). The girls' protest is categorical:

> "I don't want him to take her away to that house in the depths of the woods" . . . "You can get lost in that steaming city of a kitchen, cluttered with spices, cooking smells, dazzling copper pots and pans." (p. 31)

This acts as a comparison which recalls the opening lines of the book and the description of the town with its flaming furnaces as a palace of the Apocalypse.

> "The women especially are evil and they sleep in the farthest rooms in beds as big as houses"...
> "The mother died, all alone, during the early morning hours. The children asleep by the fire didn't notice. Their servant had fled away the night before and their father hadn't come back from hunting. Then he died in a foreign land. The little girl grew up." (p. 31)

And Catherine's sisters are right because everything they mention here — loneliness, boredom, solitary death while the children crouch by the fire — will be relived by Catherine in the wood panelled rooms, ("les chambres de bois"). Michel buys her a fine bed and leaves her alone in it. When she calls out in the night nobody answers; Michel and Lia are together in the other room.

The house is linked to images of darkness and fire similar to those describing the town. It is the source of the smouldering passions of Lia and Michel, the symbol of repressed sexuality. Catherine dreams of her escape from it:

> The seigniorial manor was cursed and condemned to flames. The tall building blazed to the sky, then collapased with a loud boom. A glowing splinter burned on Catherine's wrist for awhile, then disappeared completely as she moved off down the road. (p. 103)

Here is the symbolic foretelling of her crisis when she burns with fever and becomes for a brief time the guardian of the fire.

Lia is marked permanently by these colours: black, bistre and red, she is the colours of the earth, of the fire and of the house, and paints chaotic canvases in her own likeness. Disorder reigns around her. In the contrast between her and Catherine is emodied the fundamental opposition of fire and earth with air and water. Catherine is pale, the colours of the beach, shells and the sea, and seems at home in translucency. She becomes paler and more ethereal as Lia abandons her earth colours to become as black as she was as a child — unlit coals. Catherine cries out the difference between them in the night; however, in her own way, each is "dead," one snow, the other cinders.

Fire is clearly a metaphor of passion, but not a healthy love such as is suggested by the occasions when the sun is evoked in its place. The sun and rain, street and courtyard, the underwater corpse-like fragility of a princess or the rosy face of an ordinary girl, are the conflicting choices offered to Catherine.

She opened two windows, one onto the courtyard and one onto the street, and paced nervously from one to the other, like a trapped animal seeking an escape. She was trembling with cold, continually comparing the courtyard and the street in a grave and mysterious game, as if her whole life suddenly hung on some elusive balance. (p. 109)

She is, however, obliged to choose, and decides to leave the substitute castle and well-like courtyard for ever.

The third part of *The Silent Rooms* is therefore full of sunlight, the bright reds of geraniums and watermelon and the living water of the sea. Catherine's meetings with Bruno take place in a garden, on a beach and in the town — controlled, unshadowy places, the antithesis of the wet and gloomy woods where she met Michel. All seems to be for the best.

But this brings us only to the middle of the fairy story. Beauty has returned to the real world, to her peasant life and former sweetheart. The dream she inhabited with the Beast is not so easily forgotten. At the end of the novel Catherine goes back to see Michel, supposedly for the last time, but his words lead us to believe that she will return to him. Michel says of Lia, but for Catherine:

"I've spent agonizing days, waiting, in shame. But I know she always comes back; it's stronger than she is . . . One day, I think, she'll become as pure again as her bones. We'll renew the pact of our childhood and no one will reach us." (p. 165)

The pact of childhood is fairy tale lore. On this level then, we should believe in the metamorphosis of the Beast and the ultimate happiness of Beauty. However, fairy tales are notoriously double-tongued, and we would be advised to beware of this invitation to revert to the transparency of childhood which, for Beauty, must be a denial of her identity as a woman. As I remember it, the only change that comes about when the Beast is transformed into a prince is that Beauty finds that he is thereby easier to live with — no anguish or rage — so she can accept her lot. Her lot does not change. She remains in decorative idleness for the rest of her days, obeying the whims of the same master as before. Same frustation, same passiveness. And this is the only future Michel invisages: "pure as her bones" he says, and to achieve this end he and the woman who returns will pray and fast together. This is a clear denial of the flesh both in the sense of the living body and of sexuality. The woman who returns to him must be as pure as a fairy tale-believing child, a spirit who can enter his dream world — no woman of flesh and blood.

This is where Anne Hébert's story stops. Whether Beauty will return to the Beast and whether his transformation to a prince will be accomplished is left a hypothesis in the mind of any reader who recognised the pattern upon which *The Silent Rooms* is constructed. The major part of the book is concentrated upon the emotions Catherine feels as she approaches marriage and her sufferings at the hands of the Beast afterwards. It draws a very powerful image of the traditional and deliberately perpetuated situation of the totally submissive wife — a little girl brought up to believe that to marry into a richer and more powerful family necessarily brings happiness. This is a learned response (it is not for nothing that Michel meets Catherine in the school), a dream inculcated particularly into bourgeois children and is one that has caused considerable distress.

Catherine strives and strives to become a pale and delicate princess but only manages to make herself unhappy. She cannot resemble Michel and Lia because she has not had the same formation. Her childhood has been one of hard work because of her mother's death. (They did not even notice their mother's death, so little difference did it make.) But this class distinction is in fact a minor thread running through the description of a much more important phenomenon, that of the wife-object who denies her own tastes, desires, emotions, her very humanity, in order to become the living — or rather dead — image of her husband's ideal woman. And often that is the purged and polished memory of his mother. At one point, when Michel carresses Catherine we are told that "all his warmth ebbed away. Catherine remained in his arms, abandoned, like a sacrificial maiden on a stone altar" (p. 50). Perhaps on the altar of his mother's tombstone.

Ostensibly *The Silent Rooms* is the story of an unfortunate marriage made by two adolescents trapped in the separate solitudes of their unhappy childhood. Catherine and Michel, both motherless from an early age and left under the same roof as a withdrawn, fear-inspiring father, never learned to express any love or tenderness. As a result their interaction continues to recreate the pattern established in each case between them and their sisters. Michel begs Catherine to stay beside him and protect him in some degree from his terror of solitude as Lia did when together they crouched beside the fire in the huge and empty house. Catherine responds with pity to his anguished appeal as she would to that of any of her sisters. It is the only emotion she understands and knows how to express; she is trapped by it because express some emotion she must.

Michel recognises her as a mother substitute (which indeed she is, sheltering under a tree in the rain, protecting the children clustered about her) the moment he first sees her, and strikes the same pathetic note every time he wants her to stay with him from then on. And every time he gets what he wants. Catherine is, however, aware of the blind egoism of the demand. " 'But Catherine, I've hardly seen you and already you want to leave me.' Catherine felt Michel's anguish weighing down upon her like a restraining hand. But she hid the joy this gave her" (p. 22).

When Lia returns to the house with her lover, Michel becomes almost frantic. This time Catherine protests when he tries to keep her with him, but her need for contact makes her accept even the bitter position of comforter-on-demand, even while she sees the trap in which she is caught (p. 39). The scene ends with one of the most ill-omened proposals of marriage ever pronounced:

> "Catherine, stay, please, don't leave me all by myself. I'll ask your father for your hand if I must, but don't leave me all alone."
> He had articulated this final, astonishing speech slowly, each word visibly bringing him immense peace.
> Now his calm hands were caressing Catherine's neck, her waist, her throat, her face. It was as if he wanted to create, without haste or passion, a body that was soft and solid in the night. (p. 40)

Michel has found his lost mother. He tucks her into bed and sleeps in a different room, buys her beautiful clothes, jewels and furniture, sometimes caresses her "to the very edge of her underwear," usually lives a life apart from hers, except when he needs comfort, and chases her roughly away when she shows concern at noises he makes in the night: "Don't I have the right any more to some solitude, to my own life?" (p. 50). In general, his treatment of Catherine is that of a boy for his mother, even to the nice Freudianism of making love to her only after being overtly cruel — and then wallowing in shame. The first time is after she cries that he does not love her: "His long body crashed down upon her, heavily, like a tree . . . Towards morning, Catherine had become a woman. Michel collapsed at her side like a drowned man, repeating, 'you are the very devil, Catherine, you are the very devil' " (p. 54). The second is after he has slapped her:

> Michel stood before her. He dragged her to the bed and took her awkwardly, furiously . . . He would have liked to drive his shame out as one throws a girl on to the streets. Catherine was the source of his shame and, through a thousand subterfuges, he avoided being in the same room with her. (pp. 92-93)

His behaviour never varies: close physical contact, pitiful cries and total unawareness of his cruelty. Even when Catherine is seriously ill and must go away if she is to survive, he appeals to her in the same passionate terms not to leave him alone, and his response to her ultimate departure is to ask who will keep him company while Lia sleeps.

This tale of an unfortunate girl married to an egotistical and immature husband is not, however, as simple as it first appears. Michel begins looking for another mother when his sister, who has clearly been substituted into his mother's role in his affections, falls in love and, to his way of thinking, deserts him for her lover. Freudian symbolism is much in evidence. Catherine is taken to the house on the day that Lia brings her lover back there; she is not invited inside and is witness to Michel's anguish concerning what is going on inside: "He knelt beside her, his head raised towards the window, perfectly still, alert, an animal on the watch" (p. 36). Here is the little boy outside his parents' bedroom door, who then rushes away crying:

> "Driven out! I'm driven out of my own house by shame! I'll never return there now. It's all filthy and wasted and ruined . . . Filth, that's what she's become, that most inviolable of all girls. She has brought evil upon us." (p. 38)

The conflict, unresolved because of the mother's death, remains buried as long as Lia stays in the family home, devoted only to her brother. But it resurfaces violently the moment she manifests her womanhood. Michel rejects her sexuality as a resurgence of the wickedness that separates him from the woman he loves, transfers the old hurt on to her and dashes away in search of the pure, innocent, idealized woman — a child who will never become sexual and therefore will never leave him, and who is too young to die. He remains in a state of arrested development in order to maintain the vision of his mother he has been able to recreate since her death — pure as her bones.

Lia, of course, in her very sexuality, is living the emotional conflict she was left with at her father's death. We are told of his hunting rights and of wicked women, of the animals he wounds and the girls he violates. Lia's lover, in his turn, usurps the "family mansion," takes and abandons what and whom he wishes and has reduced the proud Lia to a woman who begs to be taken in for one more night. Yet, it would seem that in their relations with each other, Michel and Lia take on the characteristics of the lost desired parent. Hence Michel's cult of childhood, for within its bounds they both have and are their own parents.

Michel seeks out Catherine because of her immaturity, the immaturity and purity expressed in the opening metaphor of the novel:

> In the morning, women wiped their windows, blackened by the fierce fires of the night. Catherine's windows were spotless. (p. 3)

He always treats her as a child (when not in need of mothering) and it is the child he will miss when she announces her final departure: "What a wounded little girl I lost along the way" (p. 166).

The notion of hurt is very important, because Michel has inherited the tradition of the lords and masters, of the "seigneurs." They hunt and women are their prey. The symbolism of the opening chapter of the novel tells us of ravaged countryside, wounded animals and girls turned wicked in a single night, and also of a little boy whose father made him carry the bag of wounded birds. Michel, as we know, is the boy. He inherits the girls who are wounded (and will die) while his father takes the wicked ones. Here the division between Catherine and Lia becomes obvious; Lia carries her father's gun, Catherine is gathered in by Michel. The wound is there and so are the joint images of marriage and death: Catherine — "little one, [how] warm and eager [you are]" (p. 34) — is ready for the hunter.

She accepts her mother's role when she receives the symbolic necklace and shawl from her aunt before setting out to visit Michel:

> Catherine didn't dare touch anything. Suddenly, she inhaled a whiff of iris that pierced her heart. She buried her head in the shawl and began nibbling it so her mother's scent would enter her mouth and touch her teeth, her palate. (p. 34)

Her passionate outburst here resonates throughout the book and adds more uncertainty to an already complex situation. Catherine is mourning her mother but there also seems to be something sacrificial in her attitude. Iris is a flower that evokes death. Does Catherine foresee her life with Michel? And if so, is it through her memory of her mother that she is thus prepared? (We remember Beauty's dead mother and her role in the fairy tale.) Or is she expressing through her mother the repressed feeling she has for her father? Is the shawl she is given here the one Lia wears when Catherine is about to die, a shawl nobody has seen her in before? Whatever else they are, the mother's possessions are symbols of a joyless role the daughter must play in her turn. Lia has the same gesture, buring her face in her mother's *Book of Hours*. They seem to be seeking to breathe in all that is left to them of their mothers at a time of need, but all they find are images of death, man-dealt death, which they accept and incorporate into themselves.

When Michel does not come to meet Catherine for a while, she thinks he has forgotten her like someone long dead. Her father cries out against a call for the dead at the moment her aunt tells her that she must marry Michel, and he also goes to a wake for a young woman the evening Catherine goes to Michel's house for the first time. These are all scenes of ill-omen reinforced by the phraseology of the letter Michel sends inviting her to go: "Come quickly, the garden will die any day now, battered by wind and ice" (p. 33), and the way Anita delivers it between two huge dead leaves. (Throughout the novel the seasons mirror the emotional mood; the first part, before Catherine's marriage, taking place in the rain and mists of Autumn, the second, beginning and ending in Winter.) Catherine herself feels the sight of the house capable of turning her into a pillar of salt, and is surprised the windows have no bars.

Her response to Michel is all the more complex because the distance he keeps from her, his pain and bereavement recall those of her father who is also lost and completely walled in by his grief. In this regard she seems to be jealous of Anita, her father's sister, and it is Anita who obliges her to marry Michel on the grounds that the marriage will lessen her father's shame. (Anita is the stepmother who drives her daughter out having initiated her into death.) Ironically, Catherine finds herself in a situation parallel to the one she has left — a husband as cut off from her as her father was and his sister who drives her out once again.

Michel tries to turn Catherine into an image of purity. First he wants to paint her portrait "in monochrome, all white and scentless, pale and cool like snow, still like water in a glass" (p. 61). Then he tries to make Catherine herself as still, colourless and unemotional as a picture: "Rest your head on the back of the chair ... I don't want you to cry or laugh" (p. 61). His ideal seems to be that she should be lifeless:

> "Catherine, how strange, you look like an idol now, with your blue eyes set in black like precious stones ... She's so beautiful, this woman, that I'd like to drown her." (pp. 69-70)

and he almost manages to achieve his ideal:

> Michel approached the bed weeping. He put the covers back over her and murmured in a scarcely intelligible voice: "Catherine, are you going to die, you're so ill today? How beautiful you are, you've never been so beautiful, Catherine."
> Catherine lay thinking: "How my death pleases you, Michel,"

and she longed for the comfort of death. Michel spoke of immediately making Catherine's death mask. In her weakness Catherine dreamt that she was eating ripe peaches, alone, in an immense orchard, where thick trees cast deep shadows like holes on the warm grass. Then, as the dream continued, she felt within herself, once again, the sound of Michel's adoration mounting, mounting like a wave about to submerge her. Soon her life would be ended. She struggled against the long, elegant, weightless hands caressing her face like sensitive leaves stirred by the breeze. A distant voice repeated wearily, summoning fleeing dark powers, "Don't move, don't move, stay still, there, there, see how she rests . . . Don't move . . . Don't move . . ."

She grew limp, languid, exhausted, without strength; she was about to dissolve into a flood of tears when the voice of her delirium soared again, clear and precise, rising from the bottom of her alerted heart: "This woman is so beautiful that I'd like to drown her."

She gave a piercieng shriek, opened her eyes and saw the terrified face of Michel leaning over her. She pushed him away, hitting him squarely in the chest with both hands.

Michel drew back, startled by Catherine's violence. Lia watched him disdainfully . . . Michel did not hear Lia's words. He drew near again, seeking in vain for a glance from his wife. Catherine had sworn not to open her eyes or respond to Michel's mute pleas. Michel was claiming the complicity with death on Catherine's burning face as his right and pleasure. Michel's lost love suddenly welled up anew in her heart. She was struggling for her life against the strange love of this man. (p. 116)

It is easy to see what Michel means by "dead," and why he wants Catherine in such a state; totally passive to his will, inexistent when he does not need her, de-sexualized, making no demands of any description yet responding to all demands made, she is the ideal child-companion, virgin-mother, who will never change, never leave. She is part of his dream world, his possession, his creation, his toy. Once that situation has been achieved, he will have fulfilled the role imposed upon him by his heritage, taught to him by word of mouth like a fairy tale: "my poor little lambs, sleep in peace. Your father is all powerful, your mother is beautiful" (p. 151) and by the model given to him by his parents.

The disaster lies in the fact that the girls have the same model and therefore let themselves be deprived of life and identity. Catherine asks whether she has not purified herself enough, become pale and fine enough to be considered a lady and she receives the fairy tale reply: "You are fine, Catherine, and fair and delicate. You shall enter the seigniorial manor by the front gate and the servant will bow down to you'. (p. 68). But dream on little girl because you are still not free to go out into the sun and pick flowers or work.

Lia is not passive like Catherine, she is nonetheless equally subservient, giving her lover everything she has and accepting death in her fashion — a death through passion.

Despite the apparent importance of Michel, *The Silent Rooms* is a book of mothers and daughters; lost mothers and daughters: Catherine and her mother, Lia and hers, Aline and Marie. Because the mothers were totally absent (passive, dead, taken away, what difference does it make?) the daughters grew up with no source of experience, council, judgment on which to draw and against which to test themselves. In each case, therefore, they continue in the role which their father seems to require: Catherine remains obedient and repressed, Lia passionate and dominated —both children still. They have been raised to be victims and victims they are, bearing the burden of shame put upon them by their menfolk. And what is that shame? Man's sexuality, which he looks on as a weakness or a sin, and for which he holds woman responsible:

> One more time, Michel's embittered body, fired up with a brief glimmer of pleasure, fell upon Catherine, only to complain afterwards, like a wave that destroys as it ebbs, that love was corrupt. (p. 95)

Lia sneers at Catherine that "her humiliated body is ignorant of love. Michel's shame is upon her" (p. 95), but she also carries the weight of Michel's disgust and the humiliation her lover has made her suffer.

Neither of them has matured enough to assume her own adulthood, to understand and accept her emotions and her body. As a result, neither of them has control of her own destiny. Each is frustrated and drained by the demands of male imposed values, yet it is the women themselves who, for lack of any other experience, continue the cycle of seeking lovers who resemble their fathers, thus perpetuating the one relationship they have learned.

The weight of St. Paul and Freud is considerable in this tableau of Quebec: Lia, the wicked woman, is painted in black and the red ochres of clay and fire. She is humiliated and drags herself in the dust, withering away to a "crow burned to a cinder" at the end. She is damned because she is lustful, made evil by the sexual urges she feels and made to suffer for her delight in the flesh — a witch.

Catherine is pale and translucent, but will never achieve transparency in real life because no matter how much she effaces herself she will still tempt man to lie with her and will be held responsible for his weakness. Michel dreams of "exorcising her tender flesh" (p. 75) and it is to this end that he makes Catherine suffer — virgin and martyr. No matter how hard she tries, though, she cannot escape her destiny as temptress (and live). Michel considers her evil to the end.

If she cannot rid herself of this role, then the only solution is to assume it — not the role of temptress, but that of a fully sexual woman — and this is what Catherine seems to manage to do. By the end of her illness she has grown up and gets out of bed "as if emerging from a shadowy adolescence." (p. 129).

Aline has cared for her throughout the crisis and now continues in her mother role. Part III of *The Silent Rooms* is thus a rebirth and a second childhood for Catherine.

After rediscovering light, colours, food and her own appearance, she becomes interested in her neighbours "as if she were trying to touch the mystery of others in the night" (p. 126). Working with Aline, she also finds her origins again and thinks for the first time in a long time of her father and sisters:

> Catherine looked down at her hands and feet, which were matted with dirt. "Here I am, as black as my father at the end of a day's work!" she thought. And she prayed that she would once again be granted the grace of living humbly and gradually through the renewal of her patient body. (p. 133)

This sentiment is very different from the one expressed at the beginning of the novel when the women complain about "the sooty faces of men quick with desire" (p. 4). Now Catherine is not struggling desperately against man and his desires, but, as yet, she has no feeling of her own as she watches lovers by the sea. Immediately after this thought, she meets the young man from the next garden, Bruno, and as a result takes the step she has not been able to take before: she frees herself from Aline, who, in a fashion proper to her mother role, has been criticising Bruno and mocking Catherine's emotional state:

> "What an old witch you are, Aline. But all this will be to no avail.

I'll leave you when I want, just as I left my husband." (p. 140)

Catherine is still going from one protector to another, but at least this time she is making her own decisions and feels herself to be adult:

> Catherine stared at the woman posed before her in the mirror. She recalled the little uncultivated girl she had been when Michel had taken her and set her to ripen in his closed rooms. (p. 143)

She says "ripen" (mûrir) but death (mourir) echoes behind the original sentence, underlining the alternatives she had: to live her own life or be a shadow in someone else's.

Her initiation is finished when she relives the death of her mother in Aline's death and rids herself of the ghost retarding her development. The old woman's experience is passed on to Catherine; first in the acceptance of the departure of her "child" and the reflux of solitude, and then in the admission of suffering:

> "My heart has known much hardship, that's all I can say,"
> ... then moaned as if in a dream how all the masters had betrayed her by their lack of grandeur... That last great lady in whom I believed, Catherine, Catherine, is false like all the rest, she's a trollop ..." (p. 151)

Aline has suffered all her life from the division between the ideal and the living, loving, sexual human being — a split which she has spent most of her life perpetuating. As the perfect servant, she has been separated from her daughter, the sign of her womanhood and of her own existence; and yet the other side of her role as servant was to accept the master into her bed at his pleasure. So she treats Catherine as a child to be cared for, while refusing all expression of vitality — work, people — just as Michel did. Only at the very moment of death does she acknowledge her own life be calling for her daughter — her immortality — and Catherine, by responding to her, frees herself finally from the glass ball of her dream. Through her "mother" she has learned how to express love and tenderness. The "decaying love," (amour pourri) that festered throughout her relationship with Michel has finally drained away.

This time Catherine is setting out in a new life with assistance and support, in stark contrast to her journey to meet Michel, when her aunt proved unable to help her. The second time she is full of joy at being with living things and she does not agree to marry Bruno until after a night of love, of "painstakingly seeking delight in spots browned by the sun, in tender places of snow or moss with their secret scents" (p. 161). Gone is all sense of humiliation and shame, of temptation by the devil, impurity and stifled passion. Catherine has assumed her womanhood, the women of Quebec have shaken loose the double yoke of servitude and sin, or however else you wish to interpret the tale.

But all is not yet won. Catherine has long-conditioned reflexes of which she must rid herself, one of which is that of treating Bruno like a little boy:

> Catherine despised his bewildered air and wanted to mark that patient face, to brand his likeness to a wounded bull on his low forehead. With both her hands, she drew his head towards her. (p. 158)

Maybe I am over-reacting, but this action seems too much like the victim scenes played with Michel to be an innocent expression of tenderness in this context.

Another touch that makes me uneasy is the statement that "he carried her to bed as one carries a dying child" (p. 183). This is Bruno, the living, vital new man who eats, swims, and makes love, and yet the joint spectres of childhood and death rise up just before Catherine agrees to marry him. Michel has not been laid to rest either; his control at the very end of the book is very important indeed. His words about Lia, always coming back, are spoken to Catherine and she has no satisfactory reply to them:

> Catherine was silent. She closed her eyes for a moment, gathering up her past like someone on the verge of death and, unable to separate it from Michel's strange gifts, discovered there a poem he had taught her and replied: "A very tiny ring for the dream, Michel, only a very tiny ring." (p. 166)

This gives me the very uncomfortable feeling that Bruno and his ring are still a dream, and either he is the Beast transformed into a prince and Beauty will go on living as she did before — remember that his proposal of marriage is made in direct opposition to Catherine's desire to work: "She also spoke about the job she'd have to find on her return. 'That's for you to decide, Catherine; as for me, I'd very much like you to be my wife . . .' " (p. 158) — or we are indeed still in the middle of the story and the sick Beauty has been allowed to return home to visit her family and rediscover her sweetheart, only to return to the Beast when he is at death's door in his turn.

The sunlight and fertility are too bright, too resolute, too brittle almost, to serve as an adequate counterweight to the gloom and damp cold emanating from the previous sections. Although the third part of the novel is clearly intended to parallel the first section, to juxtapose reality to dream and disillusion and prove it superior, I find its very determination disquieting. It is a reaction against the depth of misery visible in the previous description of woman's condition, the result of a desire to express some hope, some belief in improvement, but the form it takes is, alas, the traditional sop fed to women for generations: when you find your True Love all will be well. This happy ending is the "and they all lived happily ever after" of the fairy story, and, as such, should undermine itself totally. After all, haven't we just learned what happens to little girls who dream of a prince? Yet the dream has not been exorcised fully, the unhealthy appeal of being a princess, even a captive princess, maintains its hold. The end of the book is a terrifying endorsement of the suffering it has revealed: "A tiny little ring for the dream Michel" — Just marry me and I will live out your dream. Beauty seems to accept the untransformed Beast. Fairy tale insidiousness would seem to be even more powerful than we have been taught to believe.

CHAPTER 3

"SNOW WHITE" AND *LES BELLES IMAGES* (Beauvoir)

Les Belles Images[1] is a textbook case of the well-trained princess who catches her prince and then realizes the limitations of her new position. Laurence, intelligent and aware, looks at her situation, her emotions, depression, repressions and final rejection of the traditional role imposed upon her and the concomitant accusations of hysteria in terms of a large section of society. As a result she does not remain blocked in the solitude her stand provokes and cannot be cowed into a belief that her values are so deviant that she must be at best unreasonable, at worst insane. In this she is unique amongst the heroines of this volume and her analysis of the deprivations imposed upon girls and their unfortunate results offers a very firm base from which to look at the others.

Curiously enough, when the novel was first published, it suffered from misunderstandings as great as those surrounding Laurence herself. Just like the class in which Laurence moves, the reviewers had been so conditioned (by fairy tales in childhood?) to looking at a male-oriented society that they seemed unable to grasp the major and very obvious themes of the novel. That this could have happened at all would seem surprising, given the storm raised by *The Second Sex*,[2] which had, after all, the same author, but that such incomprehension should have been professed by some of the major reviewers in France either smacks of wilful wrongheadedness or is a tribute to the power of social conditioning and our faculty of forgetting problematical issues.

Whatever the cause, *Les Belles Images*, facing a high expectation amongst its public as it was the first novel Simone de Beauvoir had written since her Goncourt prize winner, *The Mandarins* in 1954, was reviewed widely and seemed to disappoint the majority of the critics. Madeline Chapsal, for example, writes of a disappointed and confused Beauvoir who "is touching

31

she touches us."³ And other critics compare *Les Belles Images* to Françoise Sagan's novels.⁴ Most astonishing of all perhaps is a long article by Francis Jeanson (who is well-known for his friendship with Beauvoir and his book on her work), published in *Réalités* in January 1967, hence both after the publication of the novel and after the first wave of reviews. In it, he mentions only the fact that the novel is on sale and makes no further comment, yet his long article is entitled "Simone de Beauvoir comes back to the novel." Meanwhile, Simone de Beauvoir herself comments in an interview published in *Le Monde*:⁵ "I have rarely had the impression of writing such a literary work."

Clearly there is some misunderstanding between author and reader. The problem lies in the fact that *Les Belles Images* is a novel with as controversial a subject as those of the earlier novels but a more difficult task because it depends to a much larger extent on the goodwill of the reader for its effect. An unperceptive reader, or one with "bad faith" can take it to be a story for a women's magazine. (The suggestion was made openly concerning *La Femme Rompue*; Bernard Pivot called his review "Simone de Beauvoir: a real woman of letters [for lonely hearts columns]"⁶). The surface similarities between Beauvoir's novel and the stories that appear in magazines such as *Elle* are in fact quite striking because, in both, the subject is woman in a man's world. The all important difference lies in the fact that the magazine author is inculcating the prince-and-saviour ideal into yet another generation — men like Jean-Charles and Gilbert are seen as ends in themselves and women are supposed to be satisfied with a husband in lieu of a life as an individual — while Simone de Beauvoir on the contrary, is describing the growing dissatisfaction of women within this role.

In the interview quoted above, Beauvoir states:

> If I wanted to define *Les Belles Images* in a word, I would say it was a book on truth. I have been forced into writing it by the very great irritation I feel when faced with the world of lies that surrounds us. (My translation)

Further on she continues: "It is rather a work of objective denunciation. For I do not deform, I photograph and the document speaks for itself. I myself am not heard" (my translation). Only the very last sentence here is inaccurate. We do hear the author's voice, but from a distance, because the Simone de Beauvoir who comes through *Les Belles Images* is the author of *The Second Sex*. This is the crux of the attitude of the critics and of Simone de Beauvoir herself, and is the point upon which they differ. The reviewers do not consider the novel in the light of the author's previous writing and so deal with the picture of the Parisian bourgeoise in the 1960's only. For Beauvoir the book is "literary" because it is an *exemplum*, illustrating some of the statements on the condition of women made in the earlier treatise, and showing the same situations and reactions still exist in the class which is supposed to have escaped them. Certainly it is a photographic presentation of a truth brought into being by "the very great irritation" that Beauvoir feels "when faced by the world of lies that surrounds us." And these lies are not only those inherent in communications and the consumer society. *Les Belles Images* is clearly presented in the terms of its women. Let us look at them in the light of the sociological description given in Section 1, Volume 2 of *The Second Sex*, the section entitled "Situation":

> Thus what bourgeois optimism has to offer the engaged girl is certainly not love; the bright ideal held up to her is that of happiness, which means the ideal of quiet equilibrium in a life of immanence and repetition. (p. 447)

We see that young girls are brought up to expect a paradise born of marriage, so that they go into their adult life confident that the ideal that has been held up before their eyes is now in their possession. Most of their problems arise from a sense of failure and frustration when their life does not prove to be so. ·

This is the fairy tale ethic found alive and well in French society. All mothers prepare their daughters to one end: life with a prince. *Les Belles Images* calls this assumption of happiness-ever-after into question as Laurence looks at her situation in relation to that of her mother and her daughter. It is here that the correspondence between the novel and the tale "Snow White" becomes apparent. Just like the queen in the story, Dominique loses all sense of her own value as a woman as her beauty fades, and fights tooth and nail against her young rival. Also like the queen, she has fashioned her daughter in her own image. As we have seen already (Chapter 1), a good queen (mother) is a "dead" one and the major role of a queen is to "kill" her daughter too in order that she may have an acceptable role in society in her turn and may attract a husband. Laurence has been given the same initiation as Snow White and if we look at the tale and the novel closely we shall see that every means the queen uses to murder the princess is used with equal success in the novel. In both cases the living child is slowly reduced to a state of death-in-life from which she escapes with difficulty.

Snow White was, according to her mother's wish, born red, white and black: the colours of blood, snow and ebony — the embodiment of the struggle between life and death, heat and cold, passion and its lack. And yet her mother, having been deprived of all expression of vitality herself, will deliberately inflict the same deprivation upon her daughter. First she demands that the girl's blood be drained away and her heart cut from her body. Then she stifles her with tight bodice laces, will give her a poisoned comb and finally choke her with an apple. With no emotion left, stifled, with no voice, caught in the snare of her own beauty and unable to move, the princess is taken away like a hunting trophy, the perfect passive wife: a corpse in a crystal box. Touchingly beautiful, standing in the great hall the prize will bring respect, admiration and a touch of sympathy to the prince — the perfect mixture for a successful man.

Snow White's only value is that of an object treasured by a rich and powerful ruler. Like her mother before her, she has lost her status as a human being and, knowing no other life except that of slaving for the dwarfs, she will very probably turn her daughter into a lifeless work of art too. And this is the message mothers have been passing on to daughters for years in the loving act of telling the child a bedtime story. Innocently?

Simone de Beauvoir gives us an effectively modernized version of the same story in *Les Belles Images*. Dominique (the queen) has brought up her daughter to have no friends and pay no attention to troubles around her — no heart; to keep immaculately clean and tidy at all times — poisoned comb and tight laces; and to take a cold shower and do gymnastics whenever she is angry — no voice. Laurence has duly become a pretty picture (une belle image) and has married her prince. It is at the moment when she catches herself holding a knife to her own daughter's heart that she begins to analyse the traditional sequence of initiation. Having been as quiescent as Snow White in her coffin, she too is brought to life; her prince has jolted her once too often. Like her fairy tale double, she vomits the obstruction her mother put in her throat, finds her voice and with it her autonomy.

Laurence is typical of a generation of women who have been sufficiently exposed to the real world of politics and business to believe they too have a place in its action. She is restrained by the values taught to her as a child and by the negative attitudes of everybody around her. She realizes that she must overcome generations of habit and prejudice, and that the struggle will be hard because, not only is it in the interest of the male population to keep her in a subordinate position, doing the work of two people — at home and in the office — but also in the immediate interest of the old and the children to have someone devoted selflessly to them. Only later will they reap the benefit of allowing her to develop as an individual, free to make her own decisions and prepared to take the responsibility for them.

The description of the situation in all fairy tales, the situation Laurence must fight against and which could well have been intended as a prologue to *Les Belles Images*, is again to be found in *The Second Sex*:

> The male is called upon for action, his vocation is to produce, fight, create, progress, to transcend himself toward the totality of the universe and the infinity of the future; but traditional marriage does not invite woman to transcend herself with him; it confines her in immanence, shuts her up within the circle of herself. She can thus propose to do nothing more than construct a life of stable equilibrium in which the present as a continuance of the past avoids the menaces of tomorrow − that is, construct precisely a life of happiness. (p. 448)

In these two sentences we have a résumé of the novel: Jean-Charles, Gilbert, Thirion, Dufrène are struggling to create a new Europe (Common Market, industry, architecture) and their sights are on the distant future, while their women folk, if they work at all outside the home, are in radio and advertising − that is, in entertainment and security in the present. Laurence has this attitude to her work: "I am not selling wooden panels: I am selling security, success, and a touch of poetry into the bargain" (p. 28), which is a reflection of her attitude to her home also: "She felt her life around her, full, warm, a nest, a cocoon; and all that was needed was a little care to prevent anything breaking in upon this security" (p. 54). Jean-Charles, of course, fits the model quoted above perfectly:

> What with the papers, the television and presently the mundovision one lives on a planetary scale. The mistake is to suppose that the planet is the universe. Still, by '85 the solar system will have been explored... Doesn't that stir your imagination? (p. 32)

The obvious division in attitude embodied by the main couples in *Les Belles Images* has been laid out thus many years earlier and so indeed has the description of their problems:

> Woman, too, must envisage purposes that transcend the peaceful life of the home; but it is man who will act as intermediary between his wife as an individuality and the universe, he will endue her inconsequential life of contingency with human worth. Obtaining in his association with his wife the strength to undertake things,

to act, to struggle, he is her justification: she has only to put her existence in his hands and he will give it meaning. (*SS*, p. 448)

The paragraph ends "We must see how this ideal is translated into reality," and it seems that the project has been carried out twice, once in *The Second Sex* and again in the later novel, for in *Les Belles Images* we see three generations of women coping as best they can within the context of accepted male superiority and the limitations, physical and psychological, imposed upon them from childhood because of their sex. The novel is a description of one very important aspect of the problem of women: that of the relation of their upbringing to their ability to assume their position in the world, to make their own decisions and accept the full responsibility thereof.

Dominique is a classic example of a woman whose total sense of self is invested in her relationship to a man. Gilbert provides her with the status she feels she deserves, but she is utterly incapable of believing in herself for herself despite the rank she has achieved in her profession. When Laurence tries to encourage her she reacts violently:

"You think it's terrific to succeed on your own? You don't know what it means. What you have to do, what you have to put up with; above all when you're a woman. I've been humiliated all my life long. With Gilbert . . ." Dominique's voice wavered. "With Gilbert I felt I was protected: at peace at last, after all those years . . ." (p. 139)

Her reaction is partly provoked by insecurity, born, of course, of the very upbringing which gave her this attitude in the first place, and also by the knowledge that people of her generation assume that any woman of importance has achieved her station as a result of the influence of the man in her life. We remember Dominique's own remark about Jeanne Texier: "She's not particularly bright — it was her husband who made her career . . ." and Laurence's reflection "In another garden, wholly different and exactly the same, someone said, 'Dominique Langlois? It was Gilbert Mortier who made her career' " (p. 11). Her work has thus no social importance and, as she was interested in it only so far as it improved her station, it can do no more for her. In her world, "a woman without a man is a woman alone" (p. 116) for a woman has no friends of her own; all her social acquaintances are searching for contact with her man. Thus when Gilbert leaves her Dominique loses all self-respect and social status.

We find her situation described in *The Second Sex*:

> Woman is not allowed to *do* something positive in her work and in consequence win recognition as a complete person. However respected she may be, she is subordinate, secondary, parasitic. The heavy curse that weighs upon her consists in this: the very meaning of her life is not in her hands. That is why the successes and the failures of her conjugal life are much more gravely important for her than for her husband; she is before all, and often exclusively, a wife, her work does not take her out of her situation; it is from the latter, on the contrary that her work takes its value, high or low. (pp. 456-57)

Thus when Gilbert tells Laurence:

> Your mother is resilient. She's perfectly aware that a woman of fifty-one is older than a man of fifty-six. She's very much attached to her career and her social life: she'll make the best of it. (p. 57)

he is exploiting two levels of reaction simultaneously to suit his own ends. He knows as well as Dominique that she is in the position described above and that for him to stress the importance of her career is sheer hypocrisy. He also thinks that he is saying the right thing to satisfy Laurence, a working woman of the younger generation; but what he is really doing is using his male prerogative by which society (which means male society, given that women have no power or autonomy) approves his ability to attract a young bride, whether by financial or physical prowess, because, just as a woman is an object to be decorated and flaunted for her husband's self-esteem, so the husband's position determines the wife's status and as such is a triumph over the rest of her sex; this is shown clearly in the relationship between Marie-Claire (Gilbert's wife), Dominique and Louise, both in her role of Gilbert's ex-mistress and that of Patricia's mother.

From this attitude then it is a short and natural step to the time and concern Dominique devoted to her appearance and her fear of growing old — which are the first traits of character revealed in the novel:

> Dominique came nearer the looking-glass. "I look awful. At my age a woman who works all day and goes out every evening is utterly done for. I ought to sleep."
>
> Laurence examined her mother in the mirror. The perfect, the ideal picture of a woman who is aging well. Who is aging. It was a picture Dominique would not accept. For the first time she

was showing weakness — flinching. Hitherto she had taken the lot, illnesses, hard knocks, everything. And now suddenly there was panic in her eyes.

"I can't believe that one day I'll be seventy."

"There's no woman who stands up to it as well as you do," said Laurence.

"My body's all right; I don't envy anyone. But look here." She pointed to her eyes, and her neck. Obviously, she was no longer in her forties.

"You aren't in your twenties any more, obviously," said Laurence. "But lots of men prefer women who know their way about. Take Gilbert..."

"Gilbert... It's to keep him that I destroy myself going out all the time. The danger is that it may turn against me." (pp. 19-20)

And, as we have seen, Dominique is right to be afraid. She is treated like another consumer product to be disposed of when out of date or a little worn. Her fear has already been described at length by Simone de Beauvoir:

Long before the eventual mutilation, woman is haunted by the horror of growing old . . . to hold her husband and to assure herself of his protection, and to keep most of her jobs, it is necessary for her to be attractive, to please; she is allowed no hold on the world save through the mediation of some man. What is to become of her when she no longer has any hold on him? (*SS* pp. 575-76)

It is no small wonder that Dominique fights to keep Gilbert, her last chance as she says. She stands to lose everything she has built up over the years by her own efforts and also the companionship and support provided by Gilbert. She feels herself rejected, both personally and publicly, as a desirable individual and as a participant in the world around her. She must recreate an entire life with other values.

In the novel we watch the stages of her development. The Dominique Langlois of the beginning of *Les Belles Images* is the perfect hostess, the elegant business woman, half of a handsome couple. She has adapted to her roles in a man's world and is the picture of the ideal mature woman. Her true situation is indicated however by her habit of imitating others rather than having a coherent style of her own. If we accept Beauvoir's thesis that through her home and her appearance a woman realizes and expresses her very self,[7] and we remember that Jean-Charles decorated Feuverolles, then we see that Dominique is playing roles on a stage. She is trying to be a variety of women at once, and has, in fact, no real perception of herself as anything other than a reflection in her mirror — an ever fashionable picture with nothing behind it.

She uses a mirror to reflect her personal image, a man to reflect her social one, hence Gilbert must be replaced by the most socially advantageous match — her estranged husband. We see the new Dominique at the family New Year party dressed for the part of young grandmother — honey coloured jersey dress, hair more white than blond. The transformation described in *The Second Sex* is under way:

> From the day a woman consents to growing old, her situation changes. Up to that time she was still a young woman, intent on struggling against a misfortune that was mysteriously disfiguring and deforming her; now she becomes a different being, unsexed but complete: an old woman. It may be considered that the crisis of her "dangerous age" has been passed. But it should not be supposed that henceforth her life will be an easy one. When she has given up the struggle against the fatality of time, another combat begins; she must maintain a place on earth. (p. 583)

The personality and development of Dominique are thus seen to be based on those of the middle aged woman described in *The Second Sex*. She has always been annexed to a man's world and as such has never been able to be herself.

The only person aware of her anxiety and her personal void is Laurence, because Laurence senses in herself the beginnings of a similar future. Trained to create beautiful images ("les belles images") and to recognise motivation, Laurence finds that places and people decompose around her into artificial structures which are destined to produce special effects on other people, manipulating them in relation to certain socially accepted ideals. Her sharpened perception makes her observe others acutely and question her own position in which she is ill at ease.

She sees her life as a series of stages, in each of which she was obliged to conform to a model. First as a girl: "She had always been a picture. Dominique had seen to that . . . A faultless child, an accomplished adolescent, a perfect young woman. 'You were so clean-cut, so fresh, so perfect . . .' said Jean-Charles" (pp. 26-27). Then as a young woman who is not even sure why she has this particular husband: "The husband's attentive look; the young wife's pretty smile" (p. 28). "The evening rites . . . After ten years of marriage, a perfect physical understanding. Yes; but one that did not change the colour of life. Love too was smooth, hygienic and habitual" (p. 33). She thinks of herself as part of a collectivity rather than as an individual. Even her depression is not allowed to have a personal cause, proper only to Laurence — many young women go through similar crises — and she frames her anxieties and pleasures in the same generalised way: "Behold the lacerated state of the woman who goes out to work" (pp. 34-35), "Mine is the normal reaction of a woman trying to protect her daughter" (p. 37), "At the beginning she had liked him to talk about her: all women like it" (p. 72). But within this conformity, despite the success in matching the ideal set up before her, Laurence feels that something vital is missing from her life.

All of this — the various stages and dissatisfactions — is to be found in *The Second Sex*, so that Laurence is indeed right to think of herself in general terms. She and all other women have to struggle with the absence of a well defined identity and as a result with the absence of a future. In *The Second Sex* we read:

> Formerly, when still sheltered by her family, the young girl used what liberty she had in revolt and hope for change, in gaining marriage itself; now she is married, and before her there is no *other* future . . . nothing to await, nothing important to wish for . . . lost in a world where no future calls, abandoned in an icy present she becomes aware of the ennui and the flat dullness of pure and empty sham. (p. 458)

Laurence expresses the same feeling:

> It seemed to me that I had no future any more; Jean-Charles and the children had one, not me; so what was the point of keeping myself up to scratch? A vicious circle: I let myself go, I grew bored and I felt myself less and less a creature in my own personal possession. (p. 53)

To recover from this situation Laurence goes out to work — a classic solution to her problem — another alternative would have been to sanctify her domesticity as Marthe does — but at work she immediately duplicates the situation she is in at home by having an affair with Lucien. This action appears to prove her liberty but in fact provides her with a male whose opinion she can trust and who can, in time of difficulty, make her decisions for her. It is Mona who points out the likeness between the two men, and at the beginning of *Les Belles Images* Laurence defers to both of them. Each in turn fits the following description in *The Second Sex*:

> He is a demi-god endued with virile prestige and destined to replace her father: protector, provider, teacher, guide; the wife's existence is to unfold in his shadow; he is the custodian of values, the sponsor of truth, the ethical vindication of the couple. (p. 461)

And to complete the parallel Laurence states on several occasions that her father is the person she loves most in the world and that she is suffering from an unresolved oedipus complex.

Laurence's problems lie here certainly, but also in the much wider context of the ambiguous relationships a woman must entertain with all men in her life. She is supposed to see herself from the outside and to remain the passive image of a universal ideal (the princess) — as Dominique has done — but she can only manage to do this at odd moments and with a certain degree of self-irony. She does not see herself as the other in a male world — although the whole style of the novel, as it shifts back and forth from the third person to interior monologue without any warning, is a constant reminder that Laurence is both a perceiving consciousness in her own world and a perceived one in that of others — and so cannot reconcile the image imposed upon her and the individuality she needs to express. The result is a mounting hostility directed at anybody who imposes a role upon her. She has not enough confidence in herself yet to state her objections and claims openly however and allows herself to be dominated in all discussion by her husband and father. The disadvantage is again culturally produced:

> He has the advantage of superior culture or, at any rate, professional training; since adolescence he has taken an interest in world affairs . . . that is, the average man has the technique of reasoning, a feeling for facts and experience, some critical sense.
>
> This is what a great many young women lack. Even if they have read . . . it is not that through mental defect they are unable to reason properly, it is rather that experience has not held them to strict reasoning; for them thought is an amusement rather than an instrument; even though intelligent, sensitive, sincere, they are unable to state their views and draw conclusions, for lack of intellectual technique. That is why their husbands . . . will easily dominate them and prove themselves to be in the right even when in the wrong. (*SS*, p. 463)

Laurence accepts this state of affairs until her family is involved. Suddenly both Dominique and Catherine have emotional upsets at the same time. Laurence tries to understand their troubles from the inside, and in the course of her efforts becomes very much aware of her situation as daughter and as mother. She sees her own future in Dominique and, because of her father's comments, her past in Catherine. Dominique prevented her from having friends and she is allowing Catherine to be separated from her friend because Catherine must measure up to Jean-Charles' desire to have a brilliant daughter. Suddenly the chain becomes clear:

> The complexes, obsessions, and neuroses of adults have their roots in the early family life of those adults; parents who are themselves in conflict, with their quarrels and their tragic scenes, are bad company for the child. Deeply scarred by their early home life, their approach to their own children is through complexes and frustrations; and this chain of misery lengthens indefinitely. (*SS*, p. 523)

On these grounds Laurence wages war on Jean-Charles. She has an opinion based on her own experience and although she cannot convince him of its truth, she is not prepared to give it up, especially when he exposes his attitude to her, his wife and to his daughter:

> So sure of his rights, so furious if we disturb the picture he has made of us, the exemplary little daughter and the exemplary young wife, and utterly indifferent to what we are in reality. (p. 162)

He is denying them the right to be anything other than images in his world and so Laurence rejects his tyranny because he has betrayed her trust. Again following the lines laid down in *The Second Sex* she makes one last attempt to shirk the responsibility implied in opposing her husband's decision, by demanding the support of her father who has always been the highest authority in her life. He fails her and she is standing irrevocably alone.

The interiorisation of her revolt produces nausea. She controls the reaction because she has always been taught to restrain her emotions — cold water and gymnastics for temper — but is less able to stifle this one because it is more violent and more important to her than ever before. Thus, she is able finally to break free of the failure syndrome that dogs so many women; she assumes her postion in the world and takes the responsibilities which are the consequences of her actions firmly upon her own shoulders. She gets what she wants and it proves surprisingly simple:

> "I'm the one who looks after Catherine. You do come in now and then. But I'm the one who brings her up and it's for me to take the decisions. I am taking them. Bringing up a child doesn't mean turning it into a pretty picture . . . If you want war, war it shall be." He thought for a while. "It is quite true that you spend much more time looking after Catherine than I do. In the last resort it's for you to decide." (pp. 220-221)

Laurence wants to give her daughter a chance she never had. It remains to be seen whether she will be able to do so, for in the novel she has controlled Catherine's experiences as much as she can rather than help her discover the world around her. She allowed Brigitte into Catherine's home, then her first reaction was to try and turn Brigitte into an image too — the episode with the pin in the skirt hem — but she did not insist when Brigitte forgot to sew her skirt and she took the girls to the *Museum of Man* which is a choice with ironic and symbolic resonance.

This symbolic thread is present throughout *Les Belles Images*. Primarily, of course, it lies in the title which is in itself a definition of the condition of woman is it is described both in *The Second Sex* and in the novel itself. The choice of persuasive communications media as the areas of work of Dominique and Laurence underlines the social pressures upon women to conform to certain norms and also the fact that women are themselves largely responsible for the perpetuation of such tyranny. And within the structure of the book each woman has an echo in another character of her own age who is a stark illustration of her potential. Dominique has a symbolic shadow in Jeanne Texier, the unsuccessful suicide. Laurence has two: her sister Marthe who is domesticity sanctified and Mona, the artist whose work is her livelihood and thus a matter that involves her deeply. For Catherine, her potential lies in a free development like Brigitte's and it is not without significance in this novel of female repression that Brigitte has no mother to impede her progress.

A fairy story with a heroine and without a stepmother-queen is so rare as to be almost inconceivable. Without her there can be no repression, no death and no prince. Brigitte has grown up without any of the restrictions imposed by the need to be a beautiful, unobtrusive image. She is untidy, free, alert, knowledgeable and, as a result, mature. The idea of being a pale reflection of or for a husband never occurs to her; like the men in the novel, she plans a useful, interesting, active life for herself in a future in which she is a full member in her own right. Brigitte has none of the symptoms of disturbance that Catherine was beginning to show — crying at night in particular — as she felt herself being forced into a pre-schizophrenic division of role from self.

This division which undermines the whole concept of self, distorts all values, prevents the formation of real relationships with others and generally turns women into perpetual victims unable even to refuse their situation, is shown in *Les Belles Images* as constantly reinforced by the family, social group, consumer propaganda, psychiatrists. And all the women adapt to it in one way or another. Each accepts her crystal coffin; Mona is the only exception. Hope is held out for the younger generation in this way. Indeed we shall see it here again because the four novels in this volume written in the 1950's and '60's all deal with aspects of the divided self, while the more recent works (see Chapter 6) reject such a personality split. Not for them the poisoned apple and subsequent death-in-life with the man who is their dream and only justification. Laurence's assumption of her rights and responsibilities and rejection of her previous subordinate role marks the achievement of an integrated self and a sense of her own worth. She will not be tormented by the loss of "femininity" that comes with age. Her sense of self is no longer dependent upon her market value as a decorative object gracing her husband's collection. Reflecting nobody, she need fear no rival in her mirror. The queen who will not kill is not dead.

CHAPTER 4

"CINDERELLA" AND *MAD SHADOWS* (Blais)[1]

Laurence fitted the pattern of the fairy tale only too well; she fulfilled all the requirements of the story and almost managed to negate her identity to the point where she became the role she had learned to play. She, however, had no inherent obstacles to face which would prevent her from being successfully conditioned. For Isabelle-Marie the situation is quite different because Isabelle-Marie is ugly — and whoever heard of an ugly princess? As ugliness in fairy tales is generally accepted to be the outward and manifest sign of wickedness, so necessarily, all her life will be marked by this convention, and she will be rejected on sight. Her story is therefore bound to go wrong despite the fact that to all intents and purposes it is a Cinderella story.

If we look at the main outline of the two stories we find that they are the same, until the marriage of the happy pair.

Cinderella does all the hard and dirty work of the household, is humiliated and ill-treated by the stepmother and sisters, mourns her dead mother, and waits. One day she goes to a ball, is chosen by a prince and her superiority over the other members of her family is established as a result of her patience, modesty, long-sufferingness and beauty. It is assumed that as she matches the model for a fairy tale princess she will live happily ever after.

Isabelle-Marie is in the same position at the beginning of *Mad Shadows*[2]; mourning her dead father, she always wears black. Her mother gives her "all the most menial chores in order to devote her life and her remaining youth to Patrice" (p. 16), criticises everything she does and never looks at her or speaks to her directly. The evening her mother announces her own marriage to Lanz, Isabelle-Marie goes to a neighbouring farm where young people are dancing. There she meets Michael, a beautiful young man with whom she lives an idyllic period of love; they marry and have a child. Michael is blind; the

45

day he regains his sight he leaves Isabelle-Marie because she is ugly. The princess is transformed instantly into a witch who destroys Patrice's beauty and Louise's land before being smitten by religious guilt and killing herself. The primary question the novel poses is that of the effect of physical appearance on human relationships and on the developing sense of self. To this end we have the contrasting examples of the beautiful Patrice and Isabelle-Marie who, we are told, is ugly. That Patrice is a boy is here immaterial; as the beauty, it is he who is brought up in his mother's image, he who is turned into a totally passive fairy tale princess. He is encouraged to be idle: a pet at Louise's feet. We learn that he soon imitates his mother in the art of painting his face:

> Ever since he was a child, Patrice had imitated his mother. Louise used a great deal of make-up. So he, too, began to play with the dazzling colours. (p. 68)

And that Louise teaches him the pleasure of looking at himself in the mirror. Narcissism is the only feeling Patrice has. He is completely empty, totally passive, a mirror reflecting his mother's emotions and desires:

> Louise . . . supplying, when necessary, the soul which was lacking. If Patrice was silent, it was because he was savouring some secret insight. If Patrice repeated the same meaningless gestures in all his games, it was because he was guided by an instinctive sense of his own beauty. He cried when he was told to, responded to her tenderness without knowing why. (p. 18)

She loves him because she can draw from his existence a double pride and pleasure: that of seeing her own beauty before her eyes and that of seeing the admiration of other people before this object she has created.

> She was trying brazenly and yet skillfully to guide the responses of this Beautiful Beast, this bewitching creature whom people pointed out in the streets. The dazzling beauty of her child filled everyone with wonder, and she savoured this, voluptuously. (p. 22)

Patrice has no autonomous existence. His only sense of his own reality comes from the sight of his image either in his mother, in the lake, or, finally, in Faust's mad singeries of his actions. He has been created to pass from hand to hand as a decorative possession, dead inside his glorious body: " 'How cold it must be beneath his skin,' she [Isabelle-Marie] thought" (p. 16). When his beauty is destroyed, he begins to develop some vestiges of self-awareness as a result of the brusque change in everybody's attitude toward him, but it is much too late; reflections are the only consciousness he knows and deprived of them he is nothing.

In Patrice the fairy tale ideal is shown up in all its hollowness. He, a mere shell, deprived even of survival instinct (allowing Isabelle-Marie to starve him while Louise is away) fits perfectly one half of the model inculcated into girl children by tradition — Patrice is the princess. (Riding is the one activity allowed him and it must compensate for all his deprivations and frustrations. It was the one offered to Catherine [*Les Belles Images*] in exchange for her friendship with Brigitte and is a recognized expression of repressed sexuality, particularly in adolescent girls.)

Louise is the aging version of the same model. Like Dominique she is terrified of growing old and losing her beauty:

> The vulgar doll was trembling.
> "And your cheek? What have you there?"
> The blemish on her cheek was like a welt on a leper, a sinister patch which threatened to destroy her. (p. 60)

Like Dominique too, she seeks a reflection of her femininity — and therefore her worth — in the man in her life. Lanz is a grotesque copy of her doll-like emptiness and of her crumbling attractiveness. His mask will fall to pieces before he dies, just as Louise's face will be eaten away gradually and Patrice's will be seared away.

The attack on the cult of beauty made in *Mad Shadows* is virulent. More blatant and more bitter than the one made in *Les Belles Images*, it follows the same line except in the situation of the heroine. Laurence is attractive; Isabelle-Marie is ugly and therefore is an automatic outcast from the system. She seems to be the other half of the fairy tale message: work hard, accept humiliations, be patient and then one day a prince will come and save you. Except, in her case, there is a postscript: if you are ugly he will leave you again, because if you are not pretty you cannot possible be good.

A great deal turns of the definition of ugliness; in Isabelle-Marie's case her certainty of ugliness comes from a comparison between the amount and way in which everyone looks at her brother and herself. She is virtually ignored; in particular, her mother avoids looking at her and never addresses her directly.

The passengers never stopped looking at Patrice. Isabelle-Marie began to blush. She felt sick to her stomach. Soon she saw nothing outside the window. A strange desire to die came over her ... Louise did not see her. Louise never really dared to look at her. Finally Isabelle-Marie buried her face in her hands.

"Mother, I have a fever."

Bewildered, physically terrified by the people around her, she heard a woman cry out, "What a handsome son you have!" And Louise, in her contented voice, answered, "Isn't he, though?" Isabelle-Marie fainted. (p. 17)

Everyone else in the novel has a partner in whom she sees herself reflected, and the reflection strengthens or even creates her sense of her own reality and selfhood, be it pleasurably or painfully; Louise has Patrice and Lanz, Patrice has Faust and, of course, Louise:

His mother again welcomed him ... With it, the child rediscovered his love for himself, his confidence in the perfect harmony of his own body. (p. 84)

Because of the reinforcement of self-esteem, shallow as it may be, given by the human partner, each individual, when alone, can draw comfort from a mirror. Pleased by her own appearance, she renews her feeling of worth in the world:

"I said that Mother does not love you any more, Patrice."
... His eyeballs were swollen with sadness and protruded in horror like those of a madman ... Patrice fled ... When he reached the lake Patrice waited for the water to bring him peace. He looked at his reflection and then rose, very slowly, holding out his arms as though trying to drink of his own beauty, drop by drop until there was no more. (p. 35)

And when he despairs that his mother has deserted him for Lanz, just before he kills Lanz, Patrice breaks Louise's mirror.

Isabelle-Marie is like her father. Since his death she has never had anyone in whom to see herself, and as a result has never developed a healthy self-esteem. Her position brings us back to the case described by Laing[3]:

The need to be perceived is not, of course, a purely visual

affair. It extends to the general need to have one's presence endorsed or confirmed by the other, the need for one's total existence to be recognised; the need, in fact, to be loved. (p. 119)

Isabelle-Marie has never been loved and therefore does not find herself lovable. She seems to have been a good, hard working child, obedient and seeking to please her mother, yet she is given no positive reinforcement, no praise and, above all, no model of what she should be, given that she is not beautiful.

She is not princess material in other ways also. It is clear that Louise loves Patrice because he is malleable ("She could make him into whatever she wanted, and this made her feel more like a mother" [p. 33]) and rejects Isabelle-Marie for her spirit, her inability or unwillingness to become a doll. All would have been well had her father lived, we are told, because Isabelle-Marie shares his love of the earth. He would have supported her aspirations and activities and provided her with a much needed reflection. All would have been well also if Louise had been able to accept her daughter's autonomy: "If only Louise had dared to love her daughter. Had Isabelle-Marie been a more simple creature, she might have grown up without malice. She had become embittered because of the passions that seethed within her" (p. 59). But, unable to tame ("kill") her daughter, by reducing her to an object like Patrice, Louise keeps the girl in a state of ontological insecurity, constantly undermining her immature sense of self further, so that Isabelle-Marie is caught in the double bind of hating and needing her mother simultaneously. Her ugliness is then the result of the emotion she sees expressed on her own features:

> Since then, bitter and diabolical reveries had haunted her every thought, until now her anguished soul was reflected, rather frighteningly, on her face. (p. 40)

In this she fits another case description given by Laing:

> On further examination it became evident that this girl's attitude to her face contained in nuclear form the central issue of her life: her relationship with her mother . . . She hated the face she saw in the mirror (her mother's). She saw, too, how full of hate for her was the face that looked back at her from the mirror; . . . She was in this respect her mother seeing the hate in her daughter's face: that is, with her mother's eyes, she saw her hate for her mother in the face in the mirror, and looked with hatred at her mother's

> hatred of herself . . . She could not tolerate the possibility, in reality, of hating her mother, nor could she allow herself to recognize the presence of hatred for herself in her mother. All that could not find direct expression and open acknowledgement in her was condensed in her presenting symptom. The central implication seemed to be that she saw her true face to be hateful (full of hate) . . . Thus, the hatred of the other person is focused on the features of him which the individual has built into his own being, and yet at the same time the temporary or prolonged assumption of another's personality is a way of not being oneself which seems to offer security. (Laing, pp. 103-104)

It is in her behaviour toward Patrice that Isabelle-Marie's dual feelings for her mother reach their clearest expression. Patrice is Louise and therefore to be hated. Isabelle-Marie is Louise and should care for him. While Louise is away, Isabelle-Marie works through both stages, first by starving her brother:

> By depriving him of food she could make him pale and wan, and this creature who had never known the touch of misery would become her puppet, her own spindly puppet. Yes, Isabelle-Marie wanted to make him ugly. (p. 25)

And then, when he is weak and she is obviously the victor, she looks after him devotedly:

> Isabelle-Marie began to rock her brother back and forth. His white body lay in her arms with one limp hand around her neck. He rested his face against her with his eyes closed . . . Abandoning himself thus to Isabelle-Marie, he was seeking the warmth of his mother. Isabelle-Marie did not try to raise him to his feet. (p. 26)

There is intense and guilty sibling rivalry in the treatment of brother by sister, which Isabelle-Marie justifies by considering Patrice an object rather than a person — an idiot without soul or mind. This attitude, which underlines once again the schizophrenic pattern, is one Isabelle-Marie is forced into to survive. Competition with Patrice for their mother's affection is too painful a thing to contemplate, so, in order to protect her own "self" Patrice must be depersonalized and thereby eliminated from the realm of human relationships. Thus his appearance remains the only means by which he causes Isabelle-Marie to feel humiliation. "The uglier she felt, the more crushed and humiliated, the more she thought about destroying her brother's unjust beauty" (p. 84). His beauty must also be destroyed then, so that he will no longer have any advantage over his sister in his relations with other people. Isabelle-Marie believes that if Patrice does not exist as a person for her and if he resembles her, then by analogy he can no longer exist for Louise either — he will thus become Isabelle-Marie's reflection both inwardly and outwardly, for she has no faith in her own existence as a person in the world. Alternatively, if he is rejected, all her fears will be confirmed. In either case Louise will be deprived of an aspect of herself and constantly reminded of the fragility of her appearance. This is Isabelle-Marie's way of denying the validity of the relationships around her and of protecting herself against the despair she feels at not being included in any of them. By denying the existence of love between the members of her family, she counterbalances the negation of existence she feels when she is deprived of love.

> She thought of the approaching marriage of this pair of dolls, a male doll and a female doll. She would have to live in the midst of this depravity — the artificial depravity of faces in the movies. How sad, she thought, they have no souls . . . And so the dolls met and were united, without needing to know one another . . . Overcome, quivering with the same anguish as that day on the train, Isabelle-Marie left the room. (p. 39)

Once again she fits one of the cases described by Laing:

> The common family sense accorded "her" no existence. Her mother had to be right, totally right. When her mother said she was bad, Julie felt this as murder. It was the negation of any autonomous point of view on her part. Her mother was prepared to accept a compliant, false self, to love this shadow, and to give it anything. She even tried to order this shadow to act as though it were a person [Patrice]. But she had never recognized the real disturbing presence in the world of a daughter with her own possibilities. (Laing, p. 193)

Isabelle-Marie is pushed toward being schizophrenic not, as in other novels, as a result of being forced into the traditional dead princess role and having her individual identity sacrificed within the general mold, but rather by being excluded from it and having her identity and her very existence denied — as Cinderella does at first. There is no place for her, she has no reflection at all.

As she does not exist for people with sight because of her face, it is natural that Isabelle-Marie should find love with someone for whom her hated face cannot make her real self invisible. Michael is blind and for him she is beautiful: "Isa-qui-est-belle." She adopts his description of her as her role: "She wanted to be in love, to be beautiful. Both of them were pure, for in them burned a longing for perfect beauty . . . She bit her lip. Yes, I will always be beautiful" (p. 42). She plays it until it fits so well that it is her real self:

> Isabelle-Marie was no longer insecure; she did not doubt her make-believe beauty. She no longer had to repeat, "I have violet eyes." She believed it. (p. 78)

She accepts her body, her lovableness as a woman and becomes an integrated whole (self and body) for the first time. Her reflection is Michael.

However, her newly acquired self-esteem is precariously dependent upon her lack of self-consciousness which is in its turn dependent upon the absence of existence-denying eyes.

> In a world full of danger, to be a potentially seeable object is to be constantly exposed to danger. Self-consciousness, then, may be the apprehensive awareness of oneself as potentially exposed to danger by the simple fact of being visible to others. (Laing, p. 109)

As soon as Michael looks at her she reverts to being her "ugly" self. And — self-fulfilling prophesy — as she is ugly because she is unloved, so, when ugly, she is unlovable. Unable to sustain her integrated identity as a loved one before a seeing public, she cannot maintain a relationship with Michael. Rejection is instantaneous and total. It is all the more devastating in that Michael is Isabelle-Marie's substitute for the dead father who cannot see her either, but in whose potential love and support she trusts utterly.

Confirmed in her belief that she is worthless, Isabelle-Marie returns to Louise and adopts her original role of "bad" daughter even more fully than before, becoming viciously destructive in her misery. As lack of beauty is the cause of her condition, she will no longer tolerate it. Hatred for Louise who denied her life now overwhelms her as any hope of being accepted has been irrevocably extinguished. Louise must be destroyed. She must be shown her true face so that her self-esteem will be shattered and she will suffer as Isabelle-Marie has suffered. To this end Isabelle-Marie scalds Patrice. Louise is then faced by the constant reminder of her own decomposition and future ugliness — which has already begun with the growth of a cancer in her cheek. In one stroke, Louise has been deprived of the self-love she refused Isabelle-Marie, Patrice has become ugly and has been deprived of love just like his sister, and Isabelle-Marie has found her reflections — reflections of her insecure sense of reality.

> Louise had lost everything, even her own body which was slowly disintegrating as the poisons of cancer continued their inexorable course. The beautiful child who once gave her such pleasure no longer existed for her, now that he was ugly. He shared the lonely fate of Isabelle-Marie . . . She [Louise] tried to preserve herself by the magic of make-up . . . It was degrading to her to have such a hopelessly disfigured monster for a son . . . Isabelle-Marie began to regain her health. She liked to laugh and sing, now that there was no beautiful face to put her to shame. (p. 102)

Louise and Patrice are no longer any threat as they have now no more existence than she has, but Isabelle-Marie is confronted with another and much more disquieting image of herself in her daughter Anne. Had Anne resembled Michael, Isabelle-Marie would have had two models of love for her child to draw on: her own love for Michael and Louise's love for Patrice — but the baby looks like Isabelle-Marie and this is disastrous from several points of view. First, as she has no love for herself at all, Isabelle-Marie cannot stand the sight of her own image, and her treatment of Anne reflects the dislike she has for herself:

> Isabelle-Marie had found the baby even more hideous than herself, and the tiny face, afflicted by the same ugliness, bearing her blood and the same tortured features, repelled her . . . Isabelle-Marie, mortified, wished she could die so that she would not have to suffer because of her daughter. (p. 81)

Her reaction is exactly the same as her mother's toward herself: this being the only model she has for mothering an "ugly" daughter, she repeats it. Thirdly, as she is excessively lucid concerning her own feelings for Louise, she is necessarily aware of the feelings Anne is developing for her and thus reinforces her own sense of unlovableness. The situation is rotten throughout and the three generations of women are trapped in it:

> "Mother, ever since I was a child you adored Patrice because

he was beautiful and hated me, the ugly one . . . You never loved me . . . Did you think I had no feelings just because I was ugly?"
. . . Anne looked at her, as curious as a grown woman about this tragedy which she was witnessing but not realizing that the tragedy was also her own.
"Those who saw me spurned me, even my husband . . . But weren't you the one who made me so ugly? Answer me, Mother. You condemn me, but my only crime was being alive. Because I do want to live, and breathe — in spite of my face . . . Mother, I despise you because you never believed in anything but your own damnable beauty. How could anyone take pity on me when my own mother rejected me? . . ."
"Leave my house, Isabelle-Marie." (p. 104-105)

Isabelle-Marie has suffered all her life from her inability to fulfill Louise's desire that she be beautiful, yet she is unable to be supportive of her daughter who has the same dream. The chain grows:

"Grandmother will be so happy to see us!" exclaimed the child. "She told me that I was beautiful."
"Hush. . ."
"She will hug me in her arms. I won't be sad any more."
. . . She was kneeling before her mirror, looking at her decayed cheek . . .
A little thinner and she would look like me, thought Isabelle-Marie . . . Isabelle-Marie saw her thus and condemned her, though she was no longer the same woman, no longer the mother who mistreated her ever since she was a child, the tireless, ever-more-powerful tormentor. Anne reached out for Isabelle-Marie's guilty arm.
"Can't we go home? I am so cold."
Isabelle-Marie smiled, a cruel and determined expression on her face. (pp. 119-20)

It is not explicitly stated in *Mad Shadows* that for Anne to be like Michael means she would have to be a boy. Beauty is not the sole property of men in the novel, instead it would seem to be a property defining anyone who is loved by a member of the opposite sex. Again, this is a delicate point to establish as the only example of non-beauty we have to draw upon is that of Isabelle-Marie. However, if we put together Patrice's oedipal rivalry with Lanz and Isabelle-Marie's loss of her father at an early age, we can perhaps assume that lack of a father-figure deprived the little girl of a counter-weight to her identity-denying relationship with her mother — Cinderella, after all, had a father to sustain her through her trials and humiliations.

If this is the case, then we are back in the pattern where women find their identity and worth only through their relationships with men. Louise's life has a purpose because she is of use to Patrice and Lanz. Isabelle-Marie has a value in the world as long as Michael loves her and a much lower value as her mother's deputy with regard to Patrice. Louise, then, having no sense of her own real worth ("She used her body with the single-minded determination of a prostitute, and had the same obsession with money" [p. 24]), can give none to her daughter. If, under these conditions, we accept Laing's statement that:

> It is out of the earliest loving bonds with the mother that the infant develops the beginnings of a being-for-itself. It is in and through these bonds that the mother "mediates" the world to the infant in the first place. (Laing, p. 190)

then we see how, in his subsequent remark, the negative phrase is the one that must apply to a girl: "The world he is given may be one he can manage to *be* in; it is possible, on the contrary, that what he is given is just not feasible for him at the time" (Laing, p. 190). She will be faced with much greater problems in becoming a whole person than her brother, even if their father is present during their childhood, because she will have to struggle against her mother's own lack of secure self-esteem which she will transmit to her daughter.

> The modern Persephone is no longer graceful, no longer divine, no longer "saved" by her mother. Demeter exists no more — and certainly not for a daughter. Whatever Earth Mother qualities women retain are lavished almost exclusively on sons and husbands. Persephone has become Cinderella, struck dumbly domestic by a Demeter turned stepmother. *This*, if anything, is the female version of exile from the earthly paradise. Fairy tale princes cannot rescue women from their exile; and mothers have become stepmothers. For this reason daughters and (step) mothers today, unlike Persephone and Demeter, are characterized by self-hatred and mutual mistrust. (Step) mothers have not prepared their daughters for pilgrimages, conquests, or reflection. They have put brooms into their hands and romantic or escapist illusions into their heads. Daughters can have no pride in their sex, which seems

to survive and fatten on its domesticity.

We must remember that the original Demeter was free and did have real powers. Demeter was not a terrible Goddess of Death but one of great earthly riches, of Life. Today, women grow up in households where adult members of their sex do not have Demeter's powers. (Step) mothers accept or glorify their servitude, sublimate their sexuality and intellect, and punish their (step) daughters when they rebel against such a role.[4]

The choices offered to girls in the society perceived by Marie-Claire Blais are those illustrated in *Mad Shadows* by Louise and Patrice and by Isabelle-Marie. If you are beautiful you can be the empty, decorative, princess-object. If you are ugly you will be universally rejected and you can go mad. Your fate is imprinted on your face. Autonomy such as is achieved by Laurence (*Les Belles Images*) or Lol Stein (*The Rapture of Lol V. Stein*) is not a possible choice.

There is one other way out: you can commit suicide. Deprived of family and home, both Isabelle-Marie and Patrice take their own lives. Patrice drowns in his own terrifying image, in the water which destroyed his beauty after providing his reflection and his pleasure:

> "How ugly I am!"
> Then, since he had nothing else in the world but the water, he plunged his head into the lake and sank after it, looking for the beautiful face. (p. 123)

Isabelle-Marie destroys herself as violently as she has destroyed everything around her, by stepping under a train. Anne remains alone to make what she can of herself in a world with neither love nor models of any kind — a new beginning, though hardly a propitious one.

The irony of the whole situation is that had Isabelle-Marie been a boy and Patrice a girl the disaster would never have occured. The whole family is locked into learned patterns of socialization which allow no scope for the individual and in which they reinforce each other's destructive bent. Obviously, at one level at least, "ugly" is a euphemism used to describe a girl who rejects her passive role and displays "masculine" behaviour. Isabelle-Marie is active, competent and takes pride in her work: "I made this bread myself so I know that it's good" (p. 22). She is proud, assertive and lucid — qualities for which she is condemned, but which are all virtues in a man. Her description of Patrice as an object, a description which is unacceptable as the attitude of a woman toward a man and which is considered a sign of her inability to cope with the world sanely, is nonetheless both an accurate reflection of the way most men think of women and have categorized them for centuries, and of the way women are portrayed in fairy tales.

Isabelle-Marie begins at the level of behaviour Laurence achieves at the end of *Les Belles Images* but, trapped in a much more rigid structure — that of Quebec rather than of France — she is undermined at every possible opportunity. Unable to translate her attitude into a positive life style, she is forced into taking a violently negative stance. Gestures are within her power, but real achievement is not, so she makes her exit in a dramatic series of destructive acts — a tragic heroine for our time, victim of the wicked stepmother, playing the negative, reversed image of the princess role to the bitter end.

CHAPTER 5

"SLEEPING BEAUTY":
THE RAPTURE OF LOL V. STEIN (Duras)

Marguerite Duras treats a theme similar to that of *Mad Shadows* in that she too deals with the effects on the self of deprivation of a loved father image. Exploration of a traumatic feeling of loss is frequent in Duras' novels, and *The Rapture of Lol V. Stein*[1] is perhaps the most powerful and complete version of them all, not only in its dealings with a personal trauma, but because it thereby reaches into a number of levels of women's development and experience. And once again a certain amount of strength lies in the fairy tale structure beneath the modern story. This time we are dealing with a "Sleeping Beauty."

Taken in the context of the fairy tale the ball at T. Beach becomes Beauty's baptism feast and Anne-Marie Stretter the uninvited fairy who robs the baby of its good fortune (Michael Richardson). Lol's convalescence in S. Tahla thus becomes the princess's childhood; her excursion to John Bedford's home and his kiss the equivalent of the meeting with the old woman in the tower and the pricked finger; the ten years of marriage the hundred years sleep (during which, in many versions of the story, the prince makes love to Beauty and she gives birth without awakening[2]). Jacques Hold is, of course, the prince whose kiss awakens the princess once again.

In the original tale the wicked fairy's curse is that the girl should die before she reaches maturity. This the good fairy transforms into a long period of dormancy terminating in marriage. The distaff drawing blood seems, in this context, to be a metaphor for menstruation, the sleep being then an adolescence as passive as those we have seen imposed upon Snow White and the other Beauty — the apparently necessary preparation for the perfect wife — and the ban on distaffs becomes the parents' attempt to prolong Beauty's childhood beyond term.

58

However, if we look back from Lol's experience which is explicitly sexual — the meeting in the tower becoming the visit to Bedford's home, his kiss taking the place of the pricked finger — we realize that the distaff is a good phallic image and that the blood drawn is that of the loss of virginity. What Beauty's father was therefore trying to prevent was his daughter's maturation into a fully sexual woman — or perhaps he was simply protecting her from a loveless rape or keeping out rivals.

In all of these cases the situation is repeated in *The Rapture of Lol V. Stein*, for just as Bedford's embrace puts Lol to sleep, so it is Hold's that awakens her to pleasure and love. The sleep is that of sexual and emotional unawareness.

While asleep, Lol is the perfect wife:

> This was the woman he loved, Lola Valerie, his serene companion, his uncomplaining sleeping beauty, his somnambulist, never obtruding, her silken body never roused, her golden presence forgotten and re-discovered as she came and went. She was gentle, he said, his gentle wife. This was how he interpreted her changeless, mute docility.
>
> Lol's running of the house in U. Bridge was rigorously methodical . . . It was as near perfection as anyone could hope to get. (p. 18)

Ideal wife, like so many others in U. Bridge, whose perfection hides a smouldering frustration:

> Lol was an imitator. But whom was she imitating? Other people, everybody, as many people as possible. In the afternoons, when she was absent, the house must have seemed like an empty stage, haunted by the echo of a soliliquy, the intonations of some obsessive passion lingering after the meaning was lost. Surely, at times, John Bedford must have sensed danger? (p. 18)

and this hidden frustration is dangerous because the wife might one day wake up, stop trying to be a reflection of the image taught to her — as Lol does — and start a new life.

John Bedford is therefore the ordinary husband whose name provides all necessary information concerning his role (for, as we see, indeed, many of the names contain a play on words and it is frequently in English[3]) — bed and ford; bed: the place for sleep and conjugal rights/rites, and ford: the place where the river runs shallowest. Thus he is put into perspective immediately, for there are a whole series of water images connected to Lol, beginning with her name Lola — *l'eau-là*, and situating her with respect to her emotions and the people in her life. For example, when Lola visits Tatiana for the first time she says that the sea is not far from her villa at U. Bridge and that without the new buildings she would have been able to see the beach from her bedroom window, yet the sea is two hours drive from U. Bridge. Clearly, as the description of her eyes indicates — "hers are like muddy pools and express nothing at present but a kind of drowsy sweetness" (p. 56) — Lol was asleep at that period, cut off from the sea, which is a metaphor for desire. Tatiana uses it explicitly when she is first invited by Lola and must therefore forego a meeting with Hold, her lover; she tells Lola "she would have to cancel her trip to the coast" (p. 59). Lola herself remains cut off from the sea until Hold takes her there himself — she stays in the railway station when she goes to T. Beach without him. Her yearning to get back to the water grows stronger with her relationship to Hold, however, and culminates in the descriptions of the beach which lead up to their lovemaking in the hotel:

>The sunlit sea is sinking, sinking, leaving behind a vast expanse of wet, bluish sand.
>She stretches out on the ground and gazes at the expanse of sand left by the ebbing sea.
>"Let's go and eat, I'm hungry." (p. 131)

>I do not have to wait long for her to wake. There are very few people here. The beach is muddy. People are bathing further up the coast, miles away . . . We contemplate one another. We have not known one another long . . . I put my arms around her and hold her close. We lie in one another's arms, speechless, unable to speak until, at the far end of the beach where the people are bathing, Lol's face is buried in my neck and she does not see it — there is a flurry. A crowd gathers round something on the beach . . . She is famished. (p. 132)

>She asks me to go and book a room. She will wait for me on the beach . . . I am with her on the beach, waiting for myself. The tide is coming in at last. It is drowning the bluish sands, little by little, slowly, rhythmically. The sands are losing their identity, merging with the sea. This is the natural order of things. Everywhere there are sands waiting to merge with the sea. As she

watches the drowning of the sands, Lol is choked with unbearable sadness. She anticipates it, she waits for it, she sees it. She recognizes it. (pp. 133-34)

When the beach is empty and muddy Lol is not yet ready for Hold, for a physical encounter, despite the desire manifest in her statements of hunger. The rising tide is the symbol of the inevitability of her sexual awakening; Lol is conscious of the loss of individuality inherent in the act:

> Lol is in a dream. She sees what is about to happen in this room occuring elsewhere and at a different time. In a different way. A thousand times over. Everywhere. Elsewhere. (p. 135)

but it grows into a sense of self — herself as Tatiana — under Hold's caress; her fear — of the arrival of the police — and inhibitions fall away; Beauty is awake.

Bedford, in contrast, provokes the shallowest of responses: comfort, affection perhaps, but no strong emotion. At this level the novel is a simple criticism of loveless marriages, and indeed, it is frequently treated as a hymn to the "coup de foudre" type of love which burns up, Racinian fashion, whoever experiences it. Lol falls in love with Michael Richardson, Richardson falls in love with Anne-Marie Stretter who shares his passion. Lol is abandoned and destroyed — a living tomb to the memory of Michael Richardson.

This brings us to the first facet of the complex part played by Tatiana Karl in Lol Stein's life. In this, the ultimate love story in which the heroine dies of love and is ressucitated, Tatiana would be the last good fairy of "Sleeping Beauty," she who was able to modify the original curse and thus prevent the princess's death. (Her name, Tatiana, certainly recalls Titania, Queen of the Fairies.) Seated by the child (Lol) when the bad fairy (Stretter) makes her entrance, she watches the child's good fortune (Richardson) drain away. And she it is who brings the prince (Hold) to the palace after the statutory number of years have gone by, and tells him about Sleeping Beauty behind the wall of vegetation.

> The woman, too, glanced at the house, but more casually, as though it were familiar to her. Lol could hear their voices but — although it was very quiet in the street — not what they were saying except for one fragment. She distinctly heard the woman say: "She may be dead, for all I know." (pp. 21-22)

Such a reading, however, leaves an unacceptable amount of unsatisfactory ambiguity in the novel. That Lol should call herself Tatiana when Hold makes love to her is comprehensible, if perhaps a little strange, but why should she insist that Hold continue his affair with Tatiana? And, above all, why should Tatiana seem jealous of Lol?

> [Tatiana to Hold] She tells me: "We won't be seeing each other again. It's over."
> "I know."
> With shame Tatiana contemplates the future, the course of events in the next few days. She hides her face in her hands.
> "It's our little Lola, I know it is."
> Once more, in the midst of tender reminiscence, she is shaken with fury.
> "It's not possible! A nut-case!" (p. 116)

To be jealous of one's protégée and to say she is mad is hardly the normal behaviour of a fairy godmother. Also, we should take into account the descriptions given of Anne-Marie Stretter and Tatiana Karl, striking enough in their similarity to suggest some degree of identification between the women:

> Anne-Marie: drifting towards them with the spent grace of a dead bird. She was thin . . . She had clothed her thin body, Tatiana clearly remembered, in a black dress, very low-cut, with an overskirt of two layers of black tulle . . . At close quarters, one could see that there was something wrong with her eyes, a discoloration of the pupils that was almost painful to look at, and this was the reason for her diffuse, unfocussed stare. (pp. 4-5)

> Tatiana: her hair, a great cloud of it, black, fine, brittle, framing a very small, pale, triangular face. Her light [grey] * eyes, in contrast, are enormous . . . She was discreetly dressed in a casual black suit. (*p. 37 Translator's addition)

Are they, in fact, one and the same, the woman who lures Lol's fiancé away and from whom she wins him back when she too comes to look like them?

> They are both [Lol and Tatiana] wearing dresses tonight, which make them look taller and slimmer. A man seeing them for the first time tonight would probably be less struck by the contrast

between them. (p. 103)

This is perhaps so, but Tatiana is rather another self to Lol than a rival.

When they were in school together they were inseparable and yet separate from the others. Tatiana sat with Lol throughout the ball, and the reactions of the two girls seem interchangeable; if anything, Tatiana has a better grasp of what is going on than Lol has.

> Lol watched him lead her on to the dance floor, as a very old woman, liberated from all commitments of the heart, watches her children growing away from her. Lovingly, it would seem . . . Nothing escaped Tatiana. She saw the new Michael Richardson advance like a victim to the sacrifice, bow, wait . . . Tatiana knew that the disorder which had overwhelmed him was now communicating itself to her. (p. 6)

Tatiana's behaviour vis-à-vis Lol is almost maternal; Anne-Marie Stretter is specifically presented as a mother — mother who forgets her daughter's existence to the point of being unaware of her departure. Are we witness to an oedipal trauma where a child feels excluded by its parents?

If we explore the hypothesis that Tatiana is, in fact, a mother figure, we find that Lol ceases to see her mother after her marriage, just as she no longer sees Tatiana, and that Lol's mother dies at about the time Tatiana marries Beugner. Also, it is the kiss exchanged by Tatiana and Hold which stirs Lol toward awakening.

> Further on, beyond the far end of the garden, they stopped. He looked about him furtively, then took the woman in his arms and kissed her with great intensity . . . Lol, in her garden, is not sure of having recognized the woman, though there had been something vaguely familiar about her features, her walk, her expression. But what of the parting kiss, guilt, intoxicating, that Lol had witnessed? Does not that also touch some chord in her memory? . . . Lol stirred. She turned over in her sleep. Lol went out. She acquired a taste for wandering. (p. 22)

In context, the memory to which Hold refers can be either a previous kiss exchanged between her mother and some man (her father) or between herself and a man, but it seems more likely that it should be one she saw received; especially if Lol's behaviour up to the previous, quoted scene of

Tatiana's jealousy be taken into account.

After she has spied on Tatiana, Lol starts going out for walks and creeping up on couples. Then she watches Tatiana and Hold at the Hôtel des Bois, makes a special effort to meet Hold — Tatiana calles her "l'intruse" (p. 73) — and charms him away from Tatiana by showing herself in situations which utilise his own desire for Tatiana, such as stroking her hair and touching her, while casting herself as the affectionate daughter. Lol is trying to understand Tatiana and displace her at the same time. When in the field behind the hotel, she thinks:

> There is a ringside seat waiting for her. Ten years ago, at T. Beach, she could not find her way to it. Where is it?
> It will not be as lavish a spectacle as the one she missed at T. Beach. What kind of show will it be? She will have to make the best of it. It is her only chance of coming a little closer to that distant shore where they live, all those other people. Coming closer to what? What is there to be found on that distant shore? (p. 39)

And we know that Hold reminds her of Richardson.

Hold gets caught in a massive transference of desire, trying to express or exorcise his emotion for Lola in his physical passion for Tatiana, and Tatiana herself feels jealous, as we have seen. Why should she call her "our little Lola" and why be ashamed if Tatiana's relationship with Lol is not maternal? Thus she makes Hold/Richardson Lol's father.

On this level it would seem that Lola, emerging from adolescence, sets herself up as her mother's direct rival. First she watches her mother with her lover:

> Tatiana Karl, in her turn, walks slowly across the lighted stage. She is naked, cloaked in her black hair. She stands still, in the centre of the rectangular frame, perhaps, directly in Lol's line of vision. She turns towards the far end of the room, where the man must be. (p. 41)

Then she asks Hold about Tatiana's performance:

> "Tatiana," she whispers . . .
> Lol, close to me, is merging, merging with Tatiana as she would like to do.* (*pp. 119-120. The last part of the translation is mine, as the published version is inaccurate.)

Lol is totally unresponsive, and only when given Tatiana's identity does she accept Hold's love-making and dissolve into Tatiana's sexual persona.

> But now she is no longer sure. The one thing she has always recognized, always proclaimed, at least ever since I have known her, is my identity [as Tatiana's lover*]. She asks:
> "Who is it?"
> She moans, imploring me to tell her. I say:
> "Tatiana Karl, for instance" . . .
> When it was over, she screamed insults at me. She begged and implored me at one and the same time to take her again, to leave her alone. Like a hunted animal, she broke away, as if to escape from the bed, from the room, and then cunningly doubled back to be recaptured. In the end, there was no difference between her and Tatiana Karl, except for her eyes, in which there was no remorse, and the names by which she called herself — Tatiana never names herself — the two names: Tatiana Karl and Lol V. Stein. (*p. 136. This is a translator's addition. In Duras' text there is mention of Lol's identity only.)

The whole sequence seems to be the working through of a previous trauma at which the book hints fairly broadly: the passion of a little girl for a father whom she feels has abandoned her for another woman (her mother or someone else — even death) because of a force she does not understand — love and desire. This loss — which would not be perceived as such by the child until it had happened, thereby clarifying Lol's avid curiosity and lack of suffering throughout the ball — is the source of much thought and dreaming as we shall see, and of action (following Bedford, for example). All of which is interpreted as suffering and madness, whereas it is rather a child's fascination with a kind of magic which is beyond its experience. We are told:

> Lol knows the hotel. She came here as a young girl with Michael Richardson . . . This is where Michael Richardson declared his love. The memory of that winter afternoon, like everything else, has become part of the S. Tahla that Lol does not know, the S. Tahla over which a coating of ice has slowly formed for Lol to glide over, day after day. (p. 39)

But as only an "oath" of love is mentioned, and as Lol met Richardson on a tennis court rather than on a beach, as he met Anne-Marie Stretter, the platonic nature of their relationship would seem to be assured. Next we are shown her reaction to the lighted window:

> She does not seek to understand the delicious lassitude which has brought her to rest here in this field. She surrenders to it. It is choking her, shaking her roughly, pitilessly. It is forcing Lol V. Stein into the abyss of sleep . . . A very faint, distant memory stirs in Lol. She felt its touch, light as a fairy's touch, soon after she lay down in the field. (p. 40)

The memory would seem to be primarily that of the ball, the final sequence of which she was not able to watch at the time because Richardson and Stretter moved out of her sight — the sequence which was now being repeated as Hold and Tatiana are not visible all the time either. This sequence, where Richardson undresses Anne-Marie and forgets Lol, is what Lol must see in order to understand what has happened to her.

> Lingeringly, he would have undressed her, and they would have travelled a long way in the time it took him to undo the fastenings of her black dress.
> I have seen Lol undressed, inconsolable, inconsolable even now.
> To Lol it was unthinkable that she should not have been present when this happened. Without her it could not have happened. She is in the shape of his hands, in the flesh of her body. She was born to see this. Others are born to die. This act, without her there to see it, is dying of thirst. It withers and falls. Lol's eyes are fixed upon its corpse. Lol is dust and ashes.
> Gradually, the tall, slender body of the other woman would have been revealed. And progressively, in inverse ratio, she would have taken Lol's place with the man at T. Beach. Within a breath of being replaced by this woman, Lol holds her breath. Slowly, as the woman's body is revealed to the man, Lol's body fades. Voluptuously, she extinguishes herself, until there is nothing of her left in all the world.
> "You. No one but you."
> This lingering disrobing of Anne-Marie Stretter, accompanied by the velvety annihilation of her own person, Lol was never able to carry through to the end. (pp. 30-31)

And she will never be able to experience it vicariously.

As with Michel in *The Silent Rooms*, we find a child outside its parent's bedroom, rejected in its immaturity. Michael Richardson left with Anne-Marie Stretter; his daughter remains faithful to her father's memory, even in marriage:

> Thus, Lol entered into a marriage which suited her admirably. She had not sought it, she had not been faced with the anguish of choice, she had not had to commit what some regard as a sin by electing another to take the place of the man who had forsaken her at T. Beach. Above all, she had been true to herself. He had stripped her of everything, and so she remained. (p. 16)

She stifles her infantile sexuality; her passion does not, therefore, transform itself naturally, and her development is blocked. Lol is separated from other people by a wall created by repressed emotion rather than by excessive love. Not until she finds a man like her father in a sexual relationship with her mother, can she begin to grow again from where she left off so many years before, taking her mother as a model for her behaviour. At one and the same time she adds the thrills of a fulfilled Electra complex to the delights of a resolved one:

> At the very moment when my hands touch Lol, I mourn the death of a nameless man, sacrificed to the immortal Michael Richardson, the man from T. Beach. His being and mine will be blended into one. All that I am and all that he was will be intermingled, pell mell, in a single entity. It will no longer be possible to separate us. I shall have no past, no present, no future. I shall lose sight of myself. I shall forget my name. Thus shall I die, slowly, little by little, forgetting more and more names, even the name of death. New highways are opening up before me. Her mouth opens as mine. Her hand on my arm, with the fingers outspread, is a relief map of the future. (pp. 78-79)

In this instance Beauty's sleep represents, not the passiveness imposed on female adolescence, but a catatonic response to a sense of abandonment.

If we consider this response further we arrive at another reading of *The Rapture of Lol V. Stein* which seems to be more complete than those previously suggested (though in no way denying their separate and collective validity) because it incorporates more of the complexities of the relationship between Tatiana and Lol than do those of the good fairy or mother figure: Tatiana is Lol's body. They are one divided self in which the emotions and the physical responses have been totally dissociated; it is not until they reach a certain maturity and also find a man who, unlike Beugner and Bedford, requires a whole partner, neither prostitute nor ideal, invisible child-servant, that they manage to come together as one personality.

The rupture is caused by Michael Richardson who gets swept off his feet by desire at the ball, and who goes far beyond Lol's capacity for response. She says later: "He had changed and so he had to go" (p. 71). The implication is that Richardson makes love to Anne-Marie Stretter all night, and that Lol can neither deal with the passion involved nor can she bear that it should come to an end.

> There is little doubt that not one of them, the man, the woman, Lol, Tatiana, had foreseen that at daybreak there must be an end. (p. 8)

> And it starts again: the close-shuttered windows of the ballroom, the nocturnal darkness within, could have contained the three of them, excluding all others. Lol is sure of it. Together, they could have prevented the coming of a new day, one day at least. (p. 29)

The ramifications here multiply. Hiding behind the green plants where Michael Richardson left her, Lol is already in her role as sleeping princess, indeed, we are told that "all three of them — including Lol — had accumulated a great weight of years, hundreds of years. The ages, which lie in wait for all who are beyond reason, had overtaken them" (p. 7). And that from the moment he leaves the Casino she is totally obsessed by the act she did not witness.

First she seems to be in shock. Her total reversion to being in her mother's care and her constant cry "These early summer dawns were deceptive, it was not really late" (p. 10) suggest that she feels too young to share Richardson's desire (it is noted on several occasions that Stretter is old). She reacts like a child for a while, then, having apparently blocked the unacceptable scene from her consciousness, wanders about in a dream. The evening with Bedford shows her playing hide and seek with her own fears and repressions.

> It was her smile that had stopped him in his tracks. She was a little shy, of course, but at the same time radiant with joy at seeing him, at seeing Everyman, coming towards her, that

night of all nights . . . She emerged from her hiding place, and went up to him . . .

"Don't be frightened. I'll see you safely home, if you like."
She did not answer. He did not repeat the offer . . .
"Where to now?"
She made an effort to keep up the pretence, looking towards the opposite pavement from which they had just crossed. But she did not point to it.
"The fact is . . ." she said. [sic]
He burst out laughing, and she joined in with zest.
"Come on, this way." Obediently she turned back with him . . . "I live not far from here," said John Bedford. "If there's anything you want to know, you have only to ask."
All he got by way of answer was a decisive "No" . . .
Still compliant, she went with him to his flat . . .
"What is it you want?"
She made a visible effort to answer him, but could not. He let it pass . . .
He could not take his eyes off her. Looking away from him, she said, with a sob:
"I have so much time. Will it never end?"
It was a cry for help. She was stifling, gasping for air. She lifted her face to his, and he kissed her. It was what she wanted. She clung to him and returned his kiss, bruising his mouth, just as if she loved him, stranger that he was. (pp. 12-15)

She behaves like a little girl; simultaneously the scene is a parody of a loveless courtship and ends with the usual request for the daughter's hand in marriage.

Throughout Lol remains totally expressionless, apparently without feelings. Her distance from other people is shown by her mistake in the layout of the garden — she made paths fanning out from the porch, but no cross-paths so that it was impossible to walk in the garden except from the house and back the same way. Presumably this is an image of her inability as yet to bring together the various feelings she has, and her desire to do so is illustrated by the fact that she works in the garden at all: the garden of Sleeping Beauty was transformed from thorns to flowers when it was time for her to wake up.

It is from within this garden that she sees and recognizes Tatiana, Tatiana kissing a man who reminds her of Richardson. At this point begins Lol's active struggle to visualize Michael's love for Anne-Marie in its full expression, and in understanding its power, to achieve the maturity to love in the same way in her turn. Going to watch Tatiana and Hold through the hotel window is a step in this direction. Tatiana feels no more love than Lol does, but she is ready to do so.

> Lol V. Stein spies on this pair of lovers. She cherishes them. She creates them. She, at any rate, is not deceived by appearances. They are not in love . . . Their union is cemented in heartlessness. It is undifferentiated, transitory, devoid of all personal preference . . . By opposing ways, they and Lol V. Stein have come to the same conclusion. They have reached it by action, discussion, lying, trial and error . . . Lol has reached it by default. (p. 38)

Just as Lol has been searching in her sleep for something to fill her emotional emptiness, so Tatiana has been seeking a physical solution.

> Her whoring body, her stigma, her *felix culpa*, hungers ceaselessly for its lost paradise. It never stops clamouring for appeasement, for fulfillment, and fulfillment was not to be found anywhere but in a hotel bed. (p. 53)

Emotional and physical development have finally drawn parallel. Tatiana must change from the "splendid prostitute" ("admirable prostituée") she has been until now, Lol from the "grown-up boarding-school girl" ("pensionnaire grandie"). They begin to draw together because of Hold, but are afraid, unused to each other and to the situation:

> Tatiana is watching Lol intently: is she going to repudiate her once and for all, or rediscover her with renewed fervour? . . .
> She seems to realize that she has allowed her attention to wander, and to be apprehensive of the consequences . . .
> "I have lovers," Tatiana says. "My free time is completely taken up with my lovers. That's how I want it" . . .
> She gets up. She tiptoes away from Tatiana, as though there were a sleeping child in the room. Tatiana goes after her, a little contrite at having, as she believes, aggravated Lol's sadness . . .
> "What do you think of our friend, Jack Hold?"
> Lol stares out into the garden. In a loud, toneless, declamatory voice, she says:
> "The best of men is dead to me. I have no views, one way or the other" . . .

> Tatiana murmers: "I've been wanting to ask you whether after all these years..." [sic] (pp. 66-67)

Then, having talked through the night of the ball one last time, the new love for Jack Hold appears. Lol expresses it first, and as we have seen, Hold comes together with Richardson at the moment he kisses her.

In love for the first time himself, he swings away from sexual activity just as Lol is moving toward it, and she has to force him to stay with Tatiana, even though on one occasion he is impotent. The man, used to the mythical division of woman into goddess and prostitute, virgin and witch, is finding that he has as much problem dealing with a whole woman, loving mind and loving body, as the woman has in uniting her emotions and actions. The night Hold kisses Lol he takes Tatiana to the Hôtel des Bois immediately afterwards, but it is not until the night spent with Lol at T. Beach that the entire woman accepts herself fully, sexually and emotionally, in her passion for Hold. The prince has kissed Sleeping Beauty; she is awake. The doctor has cured Lol V. Stein.

It is significant that Hold should be a doctor and that Lol should be described as "dingue" by Tatiana, and yet it is Tatiana who fears that Lol might be cured:

> Lol, though not very forthcoming, was quite coherent and rational. Most people would have found this reassuring, but not Tatiana. Tatiana's feelings about Lol were different from other people's. It saddened her to see Lol so much recovered. No one should ever be completely cured of the delirium of love. Moreover, in spite of her doubts about the part she herself had played in Lol's crisis, she still believed that Lol's had been an ineffable passion. (p. 50)

What Tatiana and Lol represent is, indeed, a classical schizoid case as described by R. D. Laing in *The Divided Self*. The girl has become "unembodied."

> In this postion the individual experiences his self as being more or less divorced or detached from his body. *The body is felt more as one object among other objects in the world than as the core of the individual's own being.* Instead of being the core of his true self, the body is felt as the core of a *false self*, which a detached, disembodied, "inner" true self looks on at with tenderness, amusement, or hatred as the case may be.

Such a divorce of self from body deprives the unembodied self from direct participation in any aspect of the life of the world, which is mediated exclusively through the body's perceptions, feelings and movements (expressions, gestures, words, actions, etc.). The unembodied self, as onlooker at all the body does, engages in nothing directly. Its functions come to be observations, control, and criticism vis-à-vis what the body is experiencing and doing, and those operations which are usually spoken of as purely "mental."
The unembodied self becomes hyper-conscious.
It attempts to posit its own imagos.
It develops a realtionship with itself and with the body which can become very complex. (p. 69)

The divorce of the self from the body is both something which is painful to be borne, and which the sufferer desperately longs for someone to help mend, but is also utilized as the basic means of defence. This in fact defines the essential dilemma. The self wishes to be wedded to and embedded in the body, yet is constantly afraid to lodge in the body for fear of there being subject to attacks and dangers which it cannot escape. Yet the self finds that though it is outside the body it cannot sustain the advantages that it might hope for in this position. (p. 161)

Lol is the unembodied self, Tatiana the body; the split is the defence against being unloved by Michael Richardson, plus an expression of the desire to be loved by him — a way of dealing with a world that has become threatening. Tatiana goes out looking for the kind of love he gave to Anne-Marie Stretter while Lol looks on. She is treating Tatiana as a separate entity for fear she should be rejected again, in which case Lola, the "true" self, will be protected from hurt. Tatiana is a role she plays for the outside world and which is false, a social exterior put on like a garment and which has no more to do with her "real" self, her inner core, than an actor's role has to do with her personality and beliefs, but which acts as a constant buffer between Lol and relationships with other people, so that Lol, locked into a relationship with herself, can feel safe. To borrow Laing's schema, the situation is: self — (body/other), in which the self considers itself separate from its body, and the body part of the world of the other with which the self can be in relationship, thus pretending to be in relationship with the true other — the world beyond its body. This a false situation, taking the place of the: (self/ body) — other, which is the relationship as it should be, and as it re-establishes itself at the end of *The Rapture of Lol V. Stein*, when Tatiana and Lol are joined in their love for Hold.

The Rapture of Lol V. Stein is a story of personal trauma and recovery with apparently no social overtones — a private loss. It is, however, a description of a woman whose entire well-being, entire identity, depends on her relationship with a man whom she loves; in that sense it is very much a part of the princess tradition. Lol and Tatiana are nothing more than sleepwalkers without Hold. Invisible women with boundless time. Women who have no presence for themselves and see themselves only in the sexually appraising eyes of men:

> He turned his head to stare at every unaccompanied, attractive woman in the street. Sometimes he stopped in his tracks to take a closer look. Blatantly. Each time, Lol gave a start, as though she were the one he was staring at. (p. 33)

and the remark (made by Hold) continues: "She is not the prisoner of any one body, hence her supreme ascendancy" (p. 34).

"Supreme ascendancy" indeed! So a woman's strength lies in the fact that she has no identity, just as in fairy tales. Women should be dead because, by tradition, men are raised to be necrophiliacs. No wonder Lol Stein "no longer spoke at all except to say how tedious, how inexpressibly and everlastingly tedious it was to be Lol V. Stein." No wonder "she had by this time given up waiting" (p. 10). With no fiancé on the horizon she has no future, and once married she can either keep the ideal house or take lovers — dead in the palace or dead looking for a new prince.

Neither Lol nor Tatiana talk very much we are told. Why not? Because in being invisible they are cut off from perception, experience and language — Sleeping Beauty does not talk. Deprived of the ability to articulate the relation of themselves with others, they thus remain divided: an undescribed (and therefore undefined) self and a body described from the outside by others. The split is institutionalized and perpetuated by women themselves: Lol is shut in by her mother and married to Bedford by her mother. Lol has a feeling that having a language would solve everything, but she cannot find the words she needs, the key to some kind of control over her own existence.

> Lol does not venture far beyond this minute [the end of the ball] into the unknown future. She resorts neither to memory nor to imagination. She does not think about it at all. But what she

does think is that she ought to have crossed the line dividing the known from the unknown. That was the thing she had left undone. And she believes that, had she done so, her mind and body, her supreme sorrow and supreme joy, would have merged into one, for all time. She believes that this did not happen, because there was no word for that which she had desired to bring about . . . But since there is no such word, she prefers to say nothing. (p. 29)

And here we see why Marguerite Duras chose to write the story of her woman through a male narrator. Women have not yet found their tongues; they are still treated and forced to treat each other from the outside with a man's language.

Duras' novel is a book with a disappearing centre, a book which contains its own description on two of the levels at which it functions:

This was the first thing I learnt about Lol: that to know nothing about her was to know her. One might, it seemed to me, go on to know less than nothing, less and less about Lol V. Stein. (p. 54)

Had such a word existed, it would have denoted absence and depth. It would have denoted a cavity into which every other word in the world was crammed. It could never have been spoken, but might have been intoned. Tremendous, endless, resounding like the hollow note of a gong . . . (p. 29)

It is a powerful metaphor of the state of all those women who, trapped within traditional fairy tale values, can see themselves only in a reflection of someone else, through their reflection in others, as Lol saw the sea in a mirror until she conquered her fears sufficiently to take on full identity and walk on the beach, visible at last in her own right.

···Part II···

She began again: "Then it really *has* happened, after all! And now, who am I? I will remember, if I can! I'm determined to do it!"
      (Carroll, *Through the Looking-Glass*)

Alice has blue eyes. *And red.* She opened her eyes as she went through the mirror. The rest seemingly still shielded from violence. Alive, alone in her house.
      (Irigaray: *This sex which is not one*)

"You must break the glass" said Alysse. "The Magic Circle is a Mirror. You must break the magic of the mirror."
      (Bersianik: *The Euguélionne*)

"What do you call yourself?" the Fawn said . . .
"I wish I knew!" thought poor Alice. She answered rather sadly, "Nothing just now."
"Think again," it said, "that won't do."
      (Carroll, *Through the Looking-Glass*)

CHAPTER 6

ON WITCHES:
POWER, SEXUALITY AND LANGUAGE

Once upon a time . . .
It cannot be said of the following story: "it's only a story." The tale remains true today. Most women who have woken up remember having slept, having been asleep/put to sleep.

Once upon a time . . . and upon another.
The beauties sleep in their woods, waiting for the prince to come and wake them. In their beds, in their glass coffins, in their childhood forests, like the dead. Beautiful but passive; therefore desirable: from them all mystery emanates. It is men who like playing dolls. As we have known since Pygmalion. Their old dream: to be god the mother. The best mother, the second one, she who gives second birth.
She is asleep, she is intact, eternal, absolutely powerless. He does not doubt that she has been waiting for him always.
The secret of her beauty, kept for him: she has the perfection of something finished. Something that has not yet begun. Yet she is breathing. Just enough life; and not too much. So he will kiss her. In such a way that when she opens her eyes she will see *him* only; him in place of everything, him-all.
— This dream is so satisfying! Who dreams it? Which desire finds fulfillment?
He leans over her . . . Cut. The tale is over. Curtain. Once awake, it would be quite another story. Then there would perhaps be two people. One never knows with women. And the voluptuous

simplicity of the preliminaries would no longer occur.

The harmony, the desire, the adventure, the search, all these movements precede — the arrival of the woman. And more exactly her *getting up*. She lying down he standing up. She gets up — end of dream — What follows is socio-cultural, he gives her lots of children, she spends her youth in childbirth; from bed to bed until the age when she is no longer a woman.

"Bridebed, childbed, bed of death."[1]

What Hélène Cixous is saying in this passage is that men appropriate women's power. Through a man's action — the prince waking the princess — woman is given a function in the system. Bridebed: she is the link between father and husband as symbol of the contract between social groups. Childbed: she is the link between husband and children as symbol of the continuation of the family. Bed of death: her passive role in all this. Woman is gift and possession, the communication of allegiance and power in concrete form, the touchstone of the whole system of values men in our civilization have built up between themselves and which has taken symbolic form in language.[2] She is the ultimate symbol of capitalism: produced by her father and sold in the market place, she is then consumed by her husband. And, as we see very clearly indeed, the foundation of the whole economy is sexual. Woman is the language of sexual power objectified.

Indeed, the whole picture was drawn in our very first fairy tale: the story of Adam and Eve. Father gave Eve to Adam and Adam made her with his own flesh. — A rib is a nice euphemism for an erect penis. — Adam had the right to name all things: he had language and the power that gives shape to his environment by definition and description. He also had the right to make things: reproduction through sexuality. All this he received from his father and from Eve's. (Remember the fairy tale kings who give their kingdom to their son-in-law.) Then the witch arrived in the shape of the serpent. This serpent had been exiled by the father already because she thought she was his equal and should share his power. Now was her chance to pass on the knowledge she had. She talked to Eve — the power of language again — and taught her where to get knowledge and life for herself. Eve picked the apple, and never doubting the equality of herself and Adam, she took it to him and shared it. Adam was willing enough, but father, who had already suppressed one revolution, was not prepared to risk another one. Retribution was swift. Adam learned his lesson: to survive well he must maintain the male order of things. Eve, outnumbered, was reduced to her role as we know it. Bitten by the serpent, she would give birth in pain in future; which, translated into fairy tale language gives: betrayed/ initiated painfully by her mother into the father's system, she is married to the prince. Bridebed, childbed, bed of death. Woman is supine, subservient to man economically, sexually and for her very life. An object for his manipulation. His language.

In this context it becomes very clear why Catherine, Laurence, Isabelle-Marie, and Lola have difficulty in speaking out. How are they to express themselves in a language of which they are the main elements? How can words change their own meaning? "When I use a word," Humpty Dumpty said to Alice, "it means just what I choose it to mean, neither more nor less."[3] And that is the position of women in society. Men have set up language; women find themselves able to see themselves only in terms of what men have made them mean. Staring at themselves in a mirror they feel to be faulty, how can they describe what they look like? As soon as they try to change their appearance Humpty Dumpty refuses to pay them, and they are obliged to reflect his view once more. In the looking glass or through the looking glass the relations of power in the world are still the same. Alice has no power over words whatsoever. She can never express herself in a way that gives her control over a situation because either the words escape her, or, on the rare occasion she is able to say something right, she is willfully misunderstood and deliberately confused by the male authority figure of the moment, until she sinks back into belief in her weakness and incompetence.

Mary Daly makes the same point when she writes in *Gyn/Ecology*:

> Hags know that "the whole World" is precisely the Otherworld, which is our own whirling World. In order to express this, we must not only break the spell of the spooking "we." It is necessary also to break the spell of the "I" of phallocratic language, the Evil "I" which spooks the speaker/writer each time she speaks/writes. (p. 237)

And she gives an example drawn from Monique Wittig's writing (her preface to *The Lesbian Body*[4]) and comments on the commentators thus:

> ... The "I" [*Je*] who writes is alien to her own writing at every word because this "I" [*Je*] uses a language alien to her; this "I" [*Je*] experiences what is alien to her since this "I" [*Je*] cannot be "un" ecrivain ... *J/e* is the symbol of the lived, rending experience which is m/y writing, of this cutting in two which does not constitute m/e as subject. *J/e* poses the ideological and historic question of the feminine subjects.

Such devices as Wittig's breaking of the pronouns to display the woman-breaking effects of language are helpful for bringing spooks out into the light. Interestingly, the publishers of the English translation of *Le Corps Lesbien*, although they split m/e and m/y, include an introduction which "explains" that "the typographical implausibility of splitting our [sic] English monosyllabic 'I' is obvious. It has therefore been printed throughout as 'I.' " "Obvious" to whom? As Emily Culpepper remarked, it was not necessary to settle for the slanted "I." She pointed out that the crossed "I" — with a line drawn through it — would resemble a broken or cut phallus. Thus it would have been very plausible and effective to split "our" English monosyllabic "I." Too plausible. The process of materializing the spooks of grammar in order to break their spell will require constant vigilance. (p. 327)

Indeed, as we saw in Chapter 1 of this book, *Alice Through the Looking Glass*, Adam and Eve, fairy tales, are all initiation texts preparing children for their rite of passage into adult roles: the ceremony of marriage in which, in the presence of an offical representative of the phallocratic *status quo* (priest, rabbi, civil registrar or judge) father hands over his daughter formally in a ritual coincidence of word and action, and she is received in the same manner. Her only role is to make a formal gesture of submission to the new authority. The importance of the market place, her value as merchandise and the power of language have all been re-affirmed in a ritual restatement (word-magic) that is at one and the same time the pivot and résumé of the social system. (Indeed, this is the function of all theatre [literature and art] to a greater or lesser degree. Just like a wedding, script, direction, major speaking parts, décor, and music are all in the hands of men. The girl just smiles and smiles.) Pygmalion's lovely statue, the bride has been reborn and, influenced by Christian overtones of death and rebirth, confidently expects to find herself in paradise after such a long and patient preparation — a wise virgin awakened by the saviour's coming.

The prince/husband is supposed to bring her to life then. And so he does — for the wedding. There the story ends; the exchange has been made. To find out what role is in store for our little princess afterwards we must read the story again. We find her right at the beginning; she is the dead mother of the next heroine — a virgin mother one might say. Indeed the attitude toward women in Christianity and in fairy tales is remarkably similar. The choice in each case lies between a Mary and a Mary Magdalene, sanctified virginity or vilified sex, princess/dead mother or step-mother/witch. Nowhere is there a non-polarised, non-manmade model of a female adult. Mother, witch, or princess: bad, mad or invisible. And always at man's service. "Behold the handmaid of the lord. Be it unto me according to thy will." "And they lived happily ever after."[5]

Always within man's power, women must operate within an all-pervasive, extremely coherent misogynous system in which, as adults, they have the choice between being a slave or a pariah. The former is "dead" in the sense of having been deprived of herself, of the power to define and create herself victim of a psychic execution. The latter is "dead" to society in which she has no place. Persecuted, punished and, in the not very distant past, slain in her millions because she spoke too powerfully, she is victim of a physical execution. The dead mother and the tormented witch are indeed models for our society: images of female weakness and female power.

The problem in aggravated by the sexual implications of each role. The witch is dangerous; she has the will and the power to change her surroundings and all who find themselves within her realm. She is, therefore, to be feared because she is knowledgeable − like Circé she can turn men into animals − hence sexually knowledgeable, thus, by man's decree, depraved, and depravity is madness. Any woman, then, who speaks out, who thus has control over her situation and over her children's lives, who makes choices and carries them out with authority, who recognises and fulfills her own desires, is almost certain to be found inconvenient by the men around her, and runs a great risk of being labelled eccentric or mad by them, as they attempt to diminish her sphere of influence, undermine her strength and confidence and prevent her speech from being heard. Return to the fairy tale: do not believe the witch, she will tell you lies or cast a spell on you. Her language is taboo.

The witch gathers information through her own senses and through her word-magic. "Mirror, mirror on the wall" is a way of saying that the queen has power; power to ask the right questions, to use her senses to receive answers, her brain to draw conclusions and decide on actions, power to give orders and get her will accomplished in an efficient way which has an impact upon her context. (The distinction between a witch and a step-mother seems to be that a step-mother works for men within their system while a witch is outside it.) She is aware of what she wants and able to get it − and for this she is punished at the end of the story because she is not an acceptable model in a male-oriented society. Too independent and capable, she is a potential threat and must be suppressed.[6]

Mysterious, able to transform herself totally, multiple and with multiple means of bewitchment, a witch is, in fact, the personification of the female sex organs and sexuality as they figure in the male imagination. In *Ce sexe qui n'en est pas un*[7] the psychiatrist Luce Irigaray writes:

> The *one* of the form, individual, sex organ, proper name, real meaning . . . supplants in parting and dividing this touching of at *least two* (lips) which keeps woman in contact with herself, but without any discrimination possible of what is touching what. Whence this mystery she represents in a culture which claims to enumerate everything, count everything in unities, make an inventory by individualities. *She is neither one nor two.* One can no more determine with precision that she be one person than two. She resists all adequate definition. Besides she has no "proper name." And her sex organs, which are not *one* organ, are counted as *no* organs. Negative, inverse, reverse of a single sex organ visible and morphologically designatable (even if that poses some problems as it passes from erection to detumescence): the penis.
>
> But the "thickness" of this "form," its folds as volume, its becoming bigger or smaller and also the timing of the moments when it comes into being as such, are secrets kept by the feminine. (p. 26)

Thus a woman in full possession of an awareness of herself has a more varied and different potential from that of a man; one which he fears and represses because he cannot or will not understand it, because its workings are not visible and unidirectional as are his own.

Over recent centuries then, man's public and private conditioning of woman has had as its primary aim the constriction of this multiplicity, brought about by persecution, humiliation and constant demands of submission. By these means the formally respected mother goddess has been reduced to the still feared but rejected image of the witch, and that of the virgin mother has been superimposed over both of them. Woman's sexuality, that dark unknown out of which comes new life, has been moved out of the realm of women's mysteries and transformed into a mystery of women. Jahweh sent the Holy Ghost to Mary and she bore a son — in total submission and ignorance, respectable only because Joseph agreed to marry her in spite of her condition. No pleasure, no power. Never are we told what she feels or says because the word is with God and the word is God. His mother has no access to language for herself. Woman has been separated from her own body as a source of experience, separated from her own emotions, deprived of a voice. She is a receptacle transferred from Jahwah to Joseph to Jesus, just as later the fairy tale heroine goes from father to husband (to child), and so do the heroines of the novels we have looked at so far.

> For, traditionally, woman is a current value for men, a unity of exchange between men. Therefore merchandise. Which leaves her keeper of the material whose price will be estimated according to the standard of their work and their need-desire by the "subjects": workers, merchants, consumers. The women are phallically marked by their fathers, husbands, pimps. And this stamp decides their value in sexual trade. Woman will never be more than the place of a more or less rival exchange between two men, and that included for the possession of the earth-mother. (Irigaray, pp. 30-31)

She has been reduced to the one role useful to men: motherhood. A role always written and directed by men be they priests, rabbis, psychologists, psychiatrists or gynecologists.

The split has been effected and sanctified. It is not by chance that in the New Testament we find Mary the Virgin, Mary the sister of Lazarus who sits at Jesus' feet (while Martha the working woman is set aside as inappropriate), and Mary Magdalene the sexual woman, rejected and guilty, whom Jesus accepts on condition that she give up her sexuality. The "witch" has been purified and incorpotated into the system. Woman's role is clearly defined: she must bear sons, neglect all other duties to listen to them (not to answer, we notice), let them take their pleasure with her, allow them to chastise and pardon her "guilt." Because man cannot or will not see that the Marys are one, will not allow them to be one, then the Marys must accept to live the divided self, coming together in sorrow at man's death.

Again the situation has its double in the sexual act itself as considered by Luce Irigaray:

> Woman "touches herself" all the time, without anyone being able to forbid her to do so, for her genitals consist of two lips which kiss continually. Thus, in herself, she is already two — but not divisible into ones — which affect each other.
>
> The suspension of this auto-eroticism happens by a violent break-in: the brutal separation of these lips by a rapist penis, which takes the woman away from this "auto-affection" which she needs if she is not to risk the disappearance of her pleasure in sexual relations. If the vagina must relay, *also* and *not only* the little boy's hand in order to assure a link between auto-eroticism and hetero-eroticism in coitus — *the meeting with the totally other always signifying death** — how, in the classic representation of sexuality,

will the continuation of auto-eroticism for woman be arranged? *Will she not be left in the impossible choice between a defensive virginity, timidly turned in on itself and a body open to penetration which in the "hole" of its sex organ no longer knows the pleasure of its own touch?* * The almost exclusive — and oh so anguished attention paid to the erection in western sexuality proves *how foreign the structure of imagination directing it is to the feminine. All there are there for the most part are imperatives dictated by the rivalry between males:* * the "strongest" being the one who "gets the most hardons," who has the longest, thickest, hardest penis, i.e., "who pees furthest" (cf. little boy's games). Or through the playing out of sado-masochistic fantasies directed by the relations between man and mother: desire to force, penetrate, appropriate the mystery of this belly where one was conceived, the secret of one's engendering, one's "origin." Desire-need, also, to make blood run again to revive a very old relationship — intra-uterine no doubt, but also prehistoric — with the maternal. (pp. 24-25. *my emphasis)

And again all the heroines of the novels we have looked at have followed this description; all deprived of sexual pleasure, and of self-appreciation, all split. In the novels to follow this question will be taken up, and in Irigaray's terms of death, the hole and blood, for these powerful symbols are central to the feminine imagination at the present time.

At all levels of our society man forces woman to be aware of him and not of herself, to accept his images of her in their contradictory nature and to live the contradiction. In all the novels considered in the first part of this study, we have seen the conflict lived in solitary anguish, regarded justly as a symptom of diminuation and incipient madness. Each of the heroines is multiple and is struggling to come to terms with her contrasting aspects, and then trying to express them. Beauvoir's novel gives a double recapitulation: Laurence finds her voice when the validity of her judgment is rejected. Because her awakening is intellectual rather than emotional she is able to retain her hold on speech and the authority it confers. The witch-virgin sexual division is, however, constantly present in the relationship of Dominique and Patricia to Gilbert. When Dominique finds her voice for a moment it is that of Snow White's stepmother, the rejected aging queen, and, captive of the male discourse, she finds another man through whom she can claim vicarious power rather than face the struggle to establish her own autonomy. In the other novels the sexual aspect of the divided female is the main theme: Lia and Catherine (Hébert), Isabelle-

Marie and her mother/brother (Blais), Tatiana/Anne-Marie Stretter and Lola (Duras) are polar opposites conditioned to oppose guilt to frustration in constant friction, rather than to fit together in harmonious satisfaction.

In each case the images are traditional and similar: Lia, Isabelle-Marie, Tatiana and Anne-Marie are described in terms of red and black, fire and ashes, passion and humiliation (in the case of Isabelle-Marie, ugliness also), and all are sexually awakened women living out their desires in suffering because in man's eyes (and therefore society's and literature's) they are evil. Good women have no right to self-generated desire. Catherine, Dominique/Patrice and Lola are pale and pure, associated with snow and water, clear as reflecting glass. Passive mirrors all, they offer the perfect image of the male-decreed description of his desired companion — virginal even in coitus, absent, dependent, silent — good because invisible.

> Woman, in the sexual imagination, is only a more or less complaisant support of the acting out of man's fantasies. That she should find pleasure by proxy is possible, even certain. But this is above all masochistic prostitution of her body to a desire that is not her own; which leaves her in that state of dependency to man that we know. Not knowing what she wants, ready for anything, even asking for more, as long as he "takes" her as "object" in the practice of his own pleasure. So she will not say what *she* wants. Besides, she does not know, or not any longer. (Irigaray, p. 25)

Lol Stein and Catherine are striking illustrations of this accommodating masochism. They remain sexlessly available, perfect Pygmalion statues, to be looked at in a way again described by Irigaray:

> In this logic [Greek] the prevalence of looking and discrimination of shape, of the individualization of form, is particularly foreign to feminine eroticism. Woman gets more satisfaction from touch than sight and her entry into a dominant scopic economy signifies that she will be assigned a passive role again: she will be the beautiful object to be looked at. If her body is thus rendered erotic and incited to make a double movement of exhibition and modest withdrawal to excite the pulsions of the "subject," her sex organs represent the *horror of nothing to see*. Fault in this systematization of representation and desire. "Hole" in its scoptophilic objective. That this nothing to see must be excluded, thrown out of a scene of such representation is already admitted in Greek

statuary. The woman's sex organs are simply not there: masked, sewn into their "slit." (pp. 25-26)

The clearest example of their opposite — the erotically aroused woman — is Isabelle-Marie, for Michael is blind and learns to love her by his touch. When his eyes open and he looks at her, all desire, mutual acceptance and love are destroyed by his measuring gaze. Isabelle-Marie is stripped by it of her individuality, her humanity, and is reduced to the object status of the others: a vase, aesthetically acceptable or not.

This parallel between fairy tale archetypes and undeveloped female sexuality underlying these women's novels is not a fortuitous one. Conditioning and result on one level, they are, on another, both reflections, each in its own way, of woman's subordinate role elsewhere, her lack of ability to speak for herself, of which Lola's muteness is the concrete expression. Any woman who cannot obtain a modicum of satisfaction for herself in the way she wants it when on a one to one basis with a man, who should show a little more goodwill toward her in such an intimate situation than elsewhere, is not likely to get what she wants in any other male-directed context.

More important, in both cases, as we have seen, woman is the object of exchange in a male-directed market. The fairy tale king giving away his daughter to a suitable heir or in exchange for a large treasure has his doubles in the father seeking a son-in-law to continue the family business and the pimp selling the prostitute. In both aristocratic and bourgeois circles the traffic in daughters is the hub of the whole system: aristocrats to maintain or improve their blood-line or connections, bourgeois families to increase their wealth and upward mobility toward real power. It is interesting to note that Michel Foucault juxtaposes the two, in terms of blood and sexuality, in the first volume of his history of sexuality. He sees blood as the symbol of an elite whose power was a power over death, and the current interest in and analysis of sexuality as a strategy for holding control over life. He writes:

> Generally speaking, at the junction of the "body" and the "population," sex becomes a central target for a power which is organised around the administration of life rather than the threat of death.
> Blood remained an important element in the mechanisms of power, its manifestations and rituals for a long time. For a society where the systems of alliance, the political procedures of the sovereign, the differentiation into orders and castes, the value of lineage are preponderant, for a society where famine, epidemics,

violence make death imminent, blood constitutes one of the essential values; its price comes at once from its instrumental role (ability to spill blood), its function in the order of signs (have a certain blood, be of the same blood, agree to risk one's blood), its instability (easy to spill, likely to dry up, too quick to mix, quickly susceptible to corruption). Blood society — I was going to say "sanguin": honour of war and fear of famine, triumph of death, ruler of the sword, executioners and torture, power speaks *through* blood; the latter is *a reality with symbolic function*. We are in a "sex" society, or rather, one of "sexuality": the workings of power are directed at the body, at life, at *what makes it proliferate, what reinforces the species, its vigour, its capacity to dominate or its aptitude to be used.* * Health, progeniture, race, future of the species, vitality of the social body, power speaks *about* sexuality and *to* sexuality; the latter is not mark or symbol, it is object and target. And what creates its importance is less its rarity or its instability than its insistance, its insidious presence, the fact that it is both kindled and feared everywhere. Power delineates it, gives rise to it and uses it as the proliferating meaning that must always be taken back under control so that it does not escape; it is an *effect with a meaning value.* I do not mean that a substitution of sex for blood resumes by itself the transformations that mark the beginning of our modernity. I am not trying to express the soul of two civilizations or the organizing principle of two cultural forms; I am looking for the reasons why sexuality, far from having been repressed in contemporary society, is, on the contrary, brought to the fore all the time. It is the new procedures of power elaborated in the classical period and put into practice in the XIXth century that have made our societies shift from a *symbolic system based on blood* to an *analytic system based on sexuality.* One can see that if there is something on the side of law, death, transgression, symbolic expression and sovreignity, it is blood; sexuality is on the side of the norm, knowledge, life, meaning, order and regulations. (pp. 193-195. * my emphasis)

Of course this is all within a male value system. Women's blood in childbirth could and frequently did signify death; a woman was necessary to form a blood alliance, to maintain the value of a lineage, and yet, as usual, she is the dark side of the world picture, passed over in silence. Again, with respect to sexuality, except in her submissive role as reproductive vessel, she is in no way representative of a norm, a knowledge, discipline or regulation. Indeed, as we have seen, she tends to represent just the opposite in the male imagination: a dark, silent guilt, unpredictable, untamed, unknown; reacting to her own rhythms and cycles despite all attempts to control her. (It is perhaps worth noting here that menstruation, generally referred to as a "period" in English, thus referring to these rhythms, is known as "règles" [rules] in French.) But, as Foucault discusses elsewhere, the analysis of sexuality has remained in the hands of men. Doctors and psychiatrists have repressed women through discourses on their sexuality until they have come to believe the male image and definition which allows them only one aspect of their activities at a time — to claim more is to be labelled hysterical immediately.

From neither system — blood-aristocracy or sexuality-bourgeoisie — do women have images of and for themselves that have not been provided by men. Blood is the symbol of an elite so that, for men, the concept of women with the kind of blood that is talked about with pride does not exist. Women's sexuality is also seen from the male point of view only; as a commodity for their use. It is very significant that amongst the novels we have looked at, the one dealing most exclusively with sexual awakening, *The Rapture of Lol V. Stein*, has a male narrator who recounts all Tatiana's and Lol's pleasure for them. They have no language to do it for themselves yet. Lola states her identity for herself, finds her name, at the moment when she feels herself sexually alive and a whole person, and her action suggests that she may achieve a language of description in the future. Again Irigaray defines the situation:

> The social inferiority of women is reinforced and complicated by the fact that woman has no access to language except by having recourse to "masculine" systems of representation which deprive her of her relation to herself and other women. The "feminine" is never determined except by and for the masculine, the reciprocal not being "true." (p. 81)

That the rise of the fairy tale in Western Europe should have been coincidental with the rise of the bourgeoisie in the 17th and 19th centuries comes now as no surprise. The increasing conditioning of little girls (seen not heard!) and the inflexibility of rules for women are two aspects of the same repression. The princess mask is applied by force and the independent woman rejected in the form of the witch. The myth of female weakness is strengthened and made more attractive by men to distract women from the potential inherent in the myth of female power. Women are divided more and more deeply by the images they are forced to live up to, the frustrating, imprisoning roles society creates for them.

From this situation has come the one image of themselves that all our heroines share — that of the "split personality"; the perfect façade masks a self which is seeking a very different fulfillment. Each feels shame and guilt because of this division which she has been taught to see as a failing, a weakness in herself, a symptom of madness. As she feels isolated within her problem, alienated from others, and as she fears this is what madness is, and knows that its recognition brings exclusion from society and a total reduction of her sphere of activity, she hides her anguish as long as possible. To the reader who is prepared to look, the social causes of her suffering are clearly visible, but in each case within the novel the woman is depicted as mad-in-the-eyes-of-those-around-her. This image of herself is imposed upon each heroine by a male value judgement; it takes time and courage for her to realise and accept that it is a ploy to keep her silent; that what her society stigmatises as irresponsible behaviour, for which it threatens to punish her with exclusion, is, in fact, her source of strength — and therefore dangerousness — to the men to whom she is supposed to belong. This is her independence of judgement and her expression of it in words, especially in her sexual roles of lover and mother. Madness is, indeed, man's derisive name for any speech (value system) that is not of his making, within his system of logic and acceptability and therefore under his control. Laurence realises this and shakes off her guilt and fear; Catherine and Lola emerge less consciously from their "madness" in time, but Isabelle-Marie is trapped by her reaction to an intolerable situation in such a way that, her speech having been refused, her muteness festers into violence. (As we shall see, Wittig considers violence the other essential acquisition for women, together with language, so, in her terms at least, Isabelle-Marie has taken a step as great as that of the others.)

Despite their increased awareness, the major metaphor of woman's condition for these heroines of the 1950's and early 1960's is still the idealised and idealistic, traditionally dumb martyrdom to male values of the fairy tale princess, with the shadow role of the witch lurking behind her, still a source of fear rather than liberation. However, more recently, a different attitude is emerging, bringing with it much less passive models. The weakness, madness and alienation, felt by and attributed to women, have not disappeared but, rather, they have been assumed positively by those under their yoke, who brandish them aggressively in the teeth of the creators of the master-slave situation: men.

Women are stating their right to have bodies, feelings, action and a language with which to describe themselves in their own value system. And in the stating of the right the reappropriation is taking place. As a result a new level of discourse is emerging which redefines the significance of traditional women's images. No longer being objectified, the new writers have no need to seek themselves in endless games with mirrors and reflections, with external appearance and role, with text and subtext, all those shifting subtleties which are so important in the work of women writers still feeling their way to a sense of self. The mirrors are still there but, as we shall see, they are turned to active use, becoming bridges to cross, weapons to blind men, burn them up, reveal them to themselves objectified in another's description: to reverse the world not to reflect it. Or they are there to be broken, as women shatter their old roles. By these actions the women are showing their take-over of the old images that have been used against them and reversing the direction of power as they turn the mirrors around.

The first image to be so transformed is the customary and insulting reference to woman as a hole. Previously a space, a nothingness, zero, the hole becomes the glorification of woman's power — the entrance to the Sibyl's cave.

The next is the complex symbolic reference of blood which is now joined to sexuality, thus incorporating both of the major male symbolic systems discussed by Foucault into one all-powerful woman's metaphor. Women's blood signifies maturity, sexual initiation, pleasure and birth of new life to women. To men, it has always been taboo: dangerous, impure, magic. As Mary Daly writes (again in *Gyn/Ecology*):

> The menstruating woman is called filthy, sick, unbalanced, ritually impure. In patriarchy her blood shed is made into a badge of shame, a sign of her radical ontological impurity. It is consistent with the logic of the woman-loathers' doublethink that the cessation of menstruation is also horrifying. Since every woman's entire being is fetishized by men, that is, condensed, displaced, and symbolized in her sexual organs and function, the cessation of any of these functions implies Female Power of Absence. Since the frustrated "worshipper's" desire for control is threatened, fetishized menopausal and postmenopausal women must be "kicked, stamped on, and dragged through the mud." (p. 248)

Yet blood, for men, carries the message of sovreignity and alliegiance and a soldier's death in battle for his beliefs. When the two symbolic networks come together, as inevitably they must in female writing, then the effect must be one of total dominance by an exclusive elite. When to this is added woman's assumption of her own body, her experience and description of herself, then comes a discovery of self, a self-love that has been systematically undermined in woman by man's presentation of and dealings with her, a sense of her own multiplicity, its rightness and potential. With her body, then, she achieves the measure of her sexuality and again transforms the bourgeois male system of organised, inspected reproduction beyond all recognition. Meanwhile, in the single act of self-statement woman takes equal right to power with god and man and thereby destroys the myth of female weakness men have carefully constructed for so long, causing the phallic tower of Babel to totter for a second time.

In her book *Man's World Woman's Place*[9] Elizabeth Janeway writes:

> Our present attitudes are built . . . on two myths: that of female weakness and that of female power. The latter goes deeper, was born earlier and is universal. Male or female, we have all grown up in the shadow of a powerful mother. The myth of female weakness appears to be a reaction to this frightening figure; whether by origin or simply by present need, it holds the myth of female power at bay. (p. 303)

> The ancient powerful goddess stirs now in the new form of the woman who can choose sex as well as a man can and who cannot be confined to her special place by the threat of pregnancy. She claims equality, but is that really what she wants?
> What men fear is, quite simply, that women will not stop at equality. Why should they not demand dominance? . . . The memory of the Mother Goddess recalls female power in action. (p. 307)

> No, they dominated women and enjoyed it. Why shouldn't they feel that deep, subliminal tremor which suggests that other people may like what they like and want it just as much as they do? As the myth of female weakness seems to crumble in their hands, they confront the myth of female power. What sacrifices will be demanded of them if women have their way? What do women want? (p. 309)

The question can perhaps be answered best by a closer look at the work of five writers of the past few years: Jeanne Hyvrard, Monique Bosco, Monique Wittig, Louky Bersianik and Constance Delaunay.

CHAPTER 7

AND THE FLESH WAS MADE WORD:
THE PRUNES OF CYTHERA (Hyvrard)
and *LES GUÉRILLÈRES* (Wittig)

"I will tell you the fractured self."

The Prunes of Cythera[1] is the summation of the previous novels; it is the monologue of a mad woman, Jeanne, who finds in herself the histories and personalities of her grandmother, mother and child as well as herself and the negro servant, and who is searching desperately for a language in which she can express her anguish and the causes and form of her madness. She needs to arrive at a description of her identity and situation before she can escape from the confusion of opposites in which she is caught. Her madness is the language of this refusal and of her suffering. A language of her body and behaviour is all she has to use, as the word-language used by the people around her is the source of her confusion, the direct cause of the conflict between her image of herself and the image others demand of her because of a constant shift of meaning. Language has a double standard of which she is victim, for there exist at least two conflicting meanings, two usages for each word: hers and the one accepted by the consensus around her — primarily her mother, however — and they belong to totally different value systems. It is because of this problem with language that Jeanne is labelled mad.

At first, when young, she does not learn to read or write or will not speak French properly. Therefore, as she is not allowed to express herself in any other way her thoughts are impeded — silenced — by external linguistically based control until she refuses to speak at all:

I will save you from words. Everything is clear. Speak. Be

quiet. Not those words. Your sentence is not correct. One does not say. One says. Language is an instrument. Words have an exact meaning. Father, father, help. Come now, don't teach her those words. You'll do her wrong. Now, now, that isn't pretty coming from a little girl's mouth. Try to smile instead. Speak softly. You'll make a little conversation. Above all be very polite. Be quiet. Let me have the last word. Answer when you're spoken to. Come to me and I will rid you of words. (pp. 28-29)

Clearly the acquisition of a certain sort of language and speech is a major part of learning and playing a specified role: that of the "dead Princess."

She's the one we prefer because she's the prettiest. She's the one who speaks best. Foreign languages, too. (p. 85)

It is an initiation into marriageability through which a girl is put by her mother and against which Jeanne struggles with all her strength. At first, in her "delirium" she repeats her mother's instructions:

I must say I've rarely seen anyone as aggressive as you are. You realize that if you go on like that you'll never manage to get married. You'll stay an old maid. Make an effort. Come on, speak quietly now. A woman must smile. Control yourself. You know, when your father is about to come home *I* put fresh rouge and powder on . . . Not that dress, it's not your style. You're like me, see. You're wide from here. (p. 17)

Gradually the accusation is voiced overtly for in the girl's eyes this upbringing is a deliberate and progressive mutilation. First she has her legs cut off, then is deprived of her hands and arms, followed by her mouth, tongue, voice, womb. Her body is forbidden to her. She is not allowed to dress it as she wishes, not touch it, nor, above all, talk about it for there is no accepted language, indeed, no language at all in which to do so.

. . . since I am death.
You have broken in yourself everything that could have helped me escape you one day. You've cut off my hands so that I should not touch a body. You have pierced my throat so that I should make no sound. You did not teach me to speak in case I should say no. Mother Earth, you have turned me into death

because you are time. You thought to make me your domain because they had taken everything from you . . . Mother Earth, I have come to be like you. Like all of us who have only a self, giving birth to each other for ever, in search of time, in search of everything. (p. 188)

Jeanne sees herself as an amputee, a prisoner-victim of her mother's life of frustration passed on from generation to generation. To other people, however, she is ill and her mother to be pitied.

Jeanne's confusion begins here in the multiple implications of the word mother, the polar opposite it contains. Mother is both danger and safety. She tries to kill her daughter at birth rather than let her go:

> I can't manage to be born. I don't want to be born, I don't want to let her be born. I am you. I am this body which contracts so strongly that she is stifling from it. My body squeezes in to embrace you, to stifle you, so that you will die sooner than escape me. (p. 73)

then stifles her by the love and restrictions imposed upon her. The child is the mother's only source of power, her only outlet. Her feelings and actions are translated by Jeanne into the dominant language as the abuse they are:

> Then she lay on top of me and stuffed her phallus into my mouth. Stop, mother, I'm not hungry any more. I don't want any more of the sperm of your love that's choking me. (p. 46)

Yet this same mother is the ultimate security, for she is the womb to which her daughter wishes to return. On the other hand, she refuses the comfort that is hers to give and rejects her daughter constantly.

> I call her. She is washing dishes. The blood is running . . . She is knitting. I shall never have children. I say her name. The earth trembles. But you don't come to my aid. I have called out and she has not heard me. I've called out and she hasn't answered me. (p. 64)

This rejection, felt at all levels, is here directed specifically at her daughter's sexuality. Because of her mother's lack of support, Jeanne has an abortion and loses both child and capacity to have children. This symbol of the refusal of her female status is a sign that Jeanne both refuses the kind of power her mother wields and all the social attributes of womanhood.

> A little wedding veil. Who doesn't dare to say no. Who doesn't dare to say, I want to live free. A well-brought-up young girl. Who is waiting for the solemn handing over of the keys. The official transfer of power. The enthronement of the new master. Not me. (p. 229)

By the loss of her womb is symbolized her revolt against the slavery of marriage, pregnancy and a life of domestic servitude. The symbol is double however, like the others, and is also a sign of Jeanne's lack of inner security. She has broken out of her prison and has no other place to go back to. She has shattered the old role, and all that is left is her anguish.

The only images she has of herself are the one her mother wants her to resemble and which she refuses, and the one she is which her mother rejects. The movement from the one to the other is symbolized by the passage through a mirror. Sometimes she goes back through it towards the house and safety — to her mother's desired image, sometimes away from it. The mirror is the door between Jeanne and the living. It is the door into madness which she goes through when values shift around her:

> Going through the mirror once more. The unbearable distress. Faces which deform and detach themselves. Are only theatre masks. (p. 121)

It is also the door through which her mother calls her when her lover brings her body to life, thus breaking the taboo by which she is bound.

> Your penis in the stars. Our bodies entwined in the bracken ... She can no longer do anything to stop me joining you ... My bare feet on the rocks. The caress of the earth against the soles of my feet ... I slip between her fingers little by little. And soon she will not be able to do anything more against me. Like so many women driven mad before me, I hear her clearly calling me from the other side of the mirror. But you are holding my hand. (pp. 221-22)

Thus we see that Jeanne holds her mother responsible for the lack of grasp she has on herself and the world, the ambiguity of her relationship to other people and to words which bring the anguish that finds its expression in her madness. She accuses her mother of stealing the language and pleads with her to teach her the one she needs to know, the one that was forbidden. But her mother either has no time to talk to her because of household tasks or tells her stories that add to her insecurity — that of Tom Thumb whose mother ate him — especially when she then forgets the end of the tale.

Her mother offers Jeanne two alternatives only: marriage or madness. By Jeanne's definition, to accept either is to be dead: "See, I'm dead. My brain paralysed" (p. 21). Indeed, if we examine the various uses of "dead" and "death" in the novel we find that they apply to every facet of a woman's role known to our narrator. To be mad is to be dead:

> Before death, the first time. Place Montparnasse. Why did I look suprised the first time the black horses carried me to the other side of the mirror. The red acids tore through the facades. The people became dummies in the wheel of the clock that turns the hours of my imprisonment... Afterwards, it was all very easy. One only had to let oneself slide. Into death. (pp. 127-28)

The mental hospital is called the "city of the dead." But death is also slavery, being in someone else's power, being vulnerable to atrocities and torture, be they electric shock treatment in hospital, rape or whipping by a slave driver, garments that prevent action or education that impedes thought. This is the situation of most women, and Jeanne sees them as dolls playing at being alive. Thus she is dead when she refuses to be an acceptable woman, but those who play the game are dead too. In fact, for men, women are death itself:

> But you don't know that women are death. Mother Death. Between our thighs they are trying to talk to you. They are so afraid that they say we are life. As if they want to ward you off. (p. 94)

Thus women are dead and bring death, but this truth is taboo. They are described as living and bringers of life; word magic for men, this reversal is the cause of the constant repression of women and the origin of the confusion of which Jeanne feels herself the victim and the embodiment. Thus she sees herself as the symbol of woman's condition:

> They have turned me into death. And it's to them that, trembling, they say: you are alive.

> Yes, my beloveds, I am the living-dead . . .
> Yes, my beloveds, I will reunite you. As the wave bears those who have drowned. For I am One. For we are one. Mother and daughter of ourselves. Endlessly. In the blood running from our vaginas . . . In the love we make to ourselves when we give birth . . .
> . . . I am death . . .
> . . . I will stifle you so well that you will join us again, for we are the world matrix.
> You are alive, says man to Death. (p. 189)

She will continue to be deprived of her potential power by such word-magic until she finds her own voice. Married women, slaves or mad women are one and the same; all are silent people. Hyvrard links them all constantly by the interchangeability of the women in Jeanne. Jeanne herself is treated as a "sale petit nègre" (dirty little nigger) when she speaks patois. The black servant is accused of letting the baby die and is taken to prison. Jeanne's baby dies and Jeanne accuses her mother of trying to kill her. Both mother and grandmother work like servants. The conclusion is that women are "black," women are "slaves" — inferior members of society on both counts.

The symbol slaves and women have in common is that of blood spilled; blood which carries the opposite messages of shame and pride. For the slaves it is pride when they kill their masters and so gain self-esteem in victory, shame when they are whipped and mutilated. For Jeanne pride is in her menstrual blood, proof of her womanhood, of her self. Blood which is the sign of maturity, sexuality, ability to love and to give birth. All of which are denied by her mother.

> I have my festivities, she would say then as she went to sleep happy in the dampness between her thighs. One doesn't talk about such things girl. You have your affairs, she asks, ready to mark the calendar. Shh, that isn't talked about. But mother why not parade your great joy? Why not flood the sheets with this happy blood? Daughter, you're dirty. You will be ashamed of your body, of your sex-blood.
> And I am dead. (p. 21)

And her blood becomes the blood of mutilation, of suffering, of rape and violence against her womanhood:

> The man with the motorcycle goes away leaving her in the grass. Tell me Mummy how can genitals bleed? Come now, little daughter, we don't talk about that. The man goes away buttoning his trousers. How can genitals hurt? Ask your mother... The man puts his hands on her breasts. She's frightened. She will never speak again. But you're at your most beautiful like that. The soldiers cover the body on the stretcher. Do you understand why anyone would jump out of a window. (pp. 116-17)

Women's blood bears a taboo. A source of fear and shame, it has only one acceptable place in the world of others — as a sign that the bride was a virgin — proof that the groom was not cheated in the exchange.

Blood, then, carries a variety of opposing meanings throughout the text. Death against life; abortion and birth; sexuality rejoiced in and denied. It is the sign of womanhood lived and rejected, the taboo of the body at its most powerful. To speak of blood, therefore, especially in the terms with which the book opens ("As if this blood which flows from my vulva all the time...") is to revolt against the whole established system. And blood is inevitably the symbol of revolt, both for the slaves and, above all, for Jeanne for whom her blood is the only voice that has not been taken away from her. All the symbols of the monologue come together as blood creates disorder and life. Disorder is madness and madness is the revolt against the humiliating order society and mothers together impose upon daughters. It is the refusal of a doll-like disposability in an attempt to gain a real life, to gain entrance to the forbidden garden and have access to the plum tree of Cythera: the tree of life.

> The red flood on the enamel of the bidet. Desire. Disorder and life. You are disorder, you say. Subterranean life. Broken. Shattered. Resurgent. The plum tree of Cythera threatening in the middle of the garden. (p. 120)

So we find that madness is death and also life. Life (as lived by others) is death. Death (in the form of woman in coitus) is life. The terms spin in eternal confusion, eternal clarity. Jeanne's values are different from those of the people around because in each case she looks at the situation and not at the term applied to describe it. Thus marriage is obviously slavery and "death" no matter what she is told to the contrary, and she is on her way to life by means of her "madness." Life comes when she is accepted for what she is, as herself, whole.

My body spreads wide around its pleasure. You give me back
the body she took from me . . . You free the servant in my possessed
belly . . . You accept me, mad in the terrifying greens of the tropical
forest . . . Haul me towards life. I'm not afraid any more. (p. 225)

She has a husband/lover who accepts her most of the time, but his role
too includes the oppositions found in the others. Sometimes he does not
recognize her. Sometimes they cannot communicate. Sometimes he merges
with her mother, sometimes with her father, and her father is the one person
whom she feels could have saved her from the death-madness out of which she
must now struggle. He could have told her she had a right to be alive.

Father, why didn't you tell me that you were like me and
that I could join you? I wouldn't be dead. (p. 129)

Her state of revolt — like her menstruation — is regarded as illness, and
it is hoped that she will be cured. Here again we are faced with two conflicting
definitions of the cure. The first, Jeanne's, is that she should manage to shake
free of all the sex-role conditioning inflicted upon her:

I shall not tell you I am beginning to be cured as long as I
haven't *vomited Cinderella and Munroe together*. Pierrette and the
pot of milk. Red Riding Hood going through the wood. *Sleeping
Beauty waiting for Prince Charming. Snow White doing house-
work.* And Garbo and Dietrich. All those women you brought us
up for, resigned foils, future exemplary mothers, killing themselves
trying to be. Tormented, adulterous women, fearful, betrayed
women . . . Virgins terrorized after twenty years in a cloister.
Married on the best day of their lives. Delivered of I hope it's
a son . . . *Turned into statues. Framed.* Limp rags. I shall not
say I am beginning to be cured as long as I have not spit in your
faces. (pp. 233-34. My emphasis)

The text begins and ends with the image of woman's condition as death-
in-life. It is the chronicle of the struggle to find a language to express the
refusal of this condition, a language that is not reversible, that cannot twist
to mean the opposite of the apparent meaning of the words used. "You can say
anything with words," (p. 27) Jeanne was told in her childhood, when she
refused to speak the official language. And she is still searching for her own.

The text is circular because the revolt has not been accomplished totally.

Jeanne's monologue is the monologue of her confusion. In it we hear all the voices that have made demands upon her or have given her conflicting images of herself.

> I am the cry of the mad woman being locked up, the furious one being stifled, the condemned man guillotined, the adolescent castrated . . . the girl to be married being dressed in flounces and furbelows. (pp. 48-49)

Through the broken sentences, questions, juxtapositions of words and incomplete phrases, the linguistic ambiguities of all kinds, we feel her struggle to achieve some kind of unity.

There are two indications that success is possible. The first is the story of Tom Thumb which runs as a refrain through the text:

> Tom Thumb who is lost. Tom Thumb whose mother has eaten him. You watch in the rocking chair, ready to tell me the story of Tom Thumb who collected pebbles so that he wouldn't get lost. You tell me the story of Tom Thumb eaten by his mother. But now you no longer know the end and you can't invent it. I am telling you the story of Tom Thumb who set off towards life. (p. 222)

A symbol of confusion and engulfment in the beginning, it becomes more helpful and changes totally when Jeanne takes control and tells it herself. Not only has the wicked mother been set aside, but the hero steps out toward success gained by his own efforts — words. It is interesting to note that tiny and weak as he may seem, Jeanne has chosen a male model. All the fairy tales for girls are rejected violently as part of the mother's preparation for her daughter's repression.

The second is, of course, the text itself. As a monologue by "Mad Jeanne," it is a testimony to her creation of a description of herself, no matter how chaotic. Indeed, its very disorder and apparent lack of logic is an active part of her revolt against "correct" behaviour and "correct" language. It is her refusal. She says:

> I want nothing to do with your world. Nor your logic. Even less to do with your language which has so many words missing. (p. 113)

It is also her act of self discovery in which dying takes on its full meaning of life in resurrection.

> Write to get better, write to reconcile two worlds. To finish being born to myself. Agree to die to be able to live at last. (p. 200)

Thus the old images of witch and dead princess are used once again. This time in active affirmation of woman's status of "other," Jeanne assumes the repressions and humiliations that have been woman's lot and then, in the rejection of them, emerges into an active being. If not yet a unified woman, she is at least one able to describe herself in her assumed world in her terms.

In this way she comes to a sense and expression of herself by breaking the double taboo imposed upon women through the denial of their bodies and their language. It is through a physical sense of oneself and one's own boundaries that one achieves a measure of the "outside world," and without such a measure one can neither be aware of nor articulate one's situation and status. *Alice in Wonderland* and *Alice Through the Looking Glass* are the perfect examples of each of these stages of appropriation of the world: in the former Alice keeps growing and shrinking and has no coherent concept of her physical boundaries, while in the second she is continually confused by the denial of her grasp on words by adult or male (or both) authority figures. Such is the traditional lot of women — powerlessness. Reasoning from this point we realize that what is really taboo is women's power: power to define, describe and thereby control themselves and the world around them. This is what Hyvrard is striving for, and it is what the new writers in Quebec — Monique Bosco, Denise Boucher, Nicole Brossard, Cécile Cloutier, Madeleine Gagnon and others are claiming as they also talk about bodies and texts as though they are interchangeable.[2]

Naturally enough, in order to achieve a language of their own, they must first rid themselves of the old one, and like Hyvrard they do not shed it until it has been worked through from a woman's perspective. If we pause for a moment to look at a text by Monique Bosco: "Mooring Buoy/Moored Body"[3] we find the full sequence of images touched upon already in this book: the dead body, fairy tales, princess then witch, the behaviour modification practised on girls who are objects of an economic exchange, woman's madness and finally Adam and Eve in a new garden. She writes:

> With what real, invented, imagined words should we treat

this body? This body, you said? The only body I know is the moored-body, the buoy, precious to sailors. Berth, anchor. With what ink should we conjure it up? In the depths of the sea, they let it slide down. Immobility achieved at last, reunion. *Woman's body ought to be thus at rest. Buried.** Let us once more bury the moored-body there. Let us once more take refuge in the sea-womb. There, in the hollow of wave and belly. In a ball. In stone. In the family way. In the stone family of saints. Glass ball. Slow swell. And already there's the nausea of the wave. Swirl and sway. Remorse. Re-moored. *Re-mort* . . .

Make yourself small. Be good. Be clean. Be quiet.* Be nice. Take care of your small brothers. Play little mother. Smile. Look pretty. Be quiet. Don't venture asking stupid questions. You'll know everything soon enough. Everything, I tell you. Everything and nothing.

Know what? Know nothing. Silly foolishness of the tales. Snow White and Cinderella.*

Mirror, mirror, tell me I'm the prettiest.

How fine, right and good it is that at least in the children's stories, the step-mothers, far too beautiful mothers, are already afraid of their ugly duckiling [sic] daughters . . .

When the mirror falls silent or no longer gives comforting answers, one must turn to the oracles of books. Page after page, to find the secret, the recipe, the infallible magic.

Where are the witches of old?* Our prosaical mothers only offer us examples of restraint or renouncement. After having told us time and again that we had plenty of time, they are delighted to find that in our turn our time's up. *Do your time,* like the unfortunate draftee on fatigue-duty. Then cast aside. Shelved. With some mending and embroidery to pass the remaining time, precisely, like the veterans . . .

Alas. We've all really been had.

And yet, how I've loved and tried to be like the heroines begotten by men. Those are my true models. Indeed, I must admit it. There I took my cruelest lessons. By heart, wholeheartedly. How do you escape from such a magnetic hold? There I thought I had understood how one must love, suffer, rebel, but above all conform to delightful precepts of moderation and sublimation. Not a trap or pitfall I didn't try, avidly, plunging into, head first . . .

And don't quote to me the Book of books. *God is not a*

nigger as in Ferré's songs. *God is a male** And from the beginning of time, he has known, wanted and accepted that David might defeat Goliath. And yet, David himself wasn't afraid to break the law. And after going to Bathsheba, he nevertheless dared compose this psalm for his God:
> Make me hear joy and gladness,
> That the bones which thou hast broken may rejoice.

For us, too, the hour of joy has come. The time of the wise ants is over.

It's cicadas' season. Songs and dances alternating. Never again oppressed and crushed under man's ruthless law. We are free now. Strong and courageous. Seeing all the adventures through. Free and alone. Death can indeed approach . . .
They maintain that they alone know the extent of my needs. *Everyone decides what is good for me.** I survived nevertheless. Tough little girl, tenacious and stubborn. How mulish I had to be. My very own head . . .
There is no more good little girl here, who works herself to death to make others love her, or at least accept her.

Yes, the ruthless training that comes after that must also be described. Only the men serve their apprenticeship, as they please, with the craftsman of their choice. *They break us in, chastise us, curb us.** To mould us, of course. Strange deformation, carefully graduated, like these espaliers in our grandmothers' beautiful orchards. That will give good pears, later on, luscious as one would wish, juicy and sweet. Delights for the lovers of good fare. *Similarly we are raised for the discerning consumption of the buyers of fresh meat for the coming seasons.** For now, we are being watched. Nothing escapes the eye or the ear of the gossips around us. They even finger, on occasion, to make sure that they're not being cheated about the goods. Already formed. Quite regular. Shocking inquiries. The searches of the jail matrons are not more severe. How I've hated that season. Cruel and thankless season. Years like centuries. Everything is whispered and mumbled with vulgar chuckles. Nothing's spared to break us in, to break me in. *Mater dolorosa.* Because our exasperated mothers complain about our rare outbursts. Under a bushel, the girls. Let's sing small. And don't you speak in undertones among yourselves. Who will come and get me out of this stupid demolition business? Let's watch the boys. Stealthily . . .

> *There, madness was avoided...**
> Quick, find again the innocence and strength of the first revolt. Heart throbbing, palms bared, *move as if it were the dawn of the first morning and the creation of another world in a garden made only in our own and radiant image.** (*my emphasis)

All the major steps by which women have been controlled are passed in review to enable the author to arrive finally at a new world created in *her* image this time:

> Quick, find again the innocence and strength of the first revolt. Heart throbbing, palms bared, move as if it were the dawn of the first morning and the creation of another world in a garden made only in our own and radiant image.

Monique Bosco is struggling against fairy tale stereotyping but is still caught to a certain extent within the net of male-given descriptions, still caught in the old system and its language, as is Hyvrard. Monique Wittig is the first woman to challenge and take over the old texts and transform them into a new vision and a new language for women in *Les Guérillères* (The Guerilla Women).

LES GUÉRILLÈRES

The women say, unhappy one, men have expelled you from the world of symbols and yet they have given you names, they have called you slave, you unhappy slave. Masters, they have exercised their rights as masters. They write, of their authority to accord names, that it goes back so far that the origin of language itself may be considered an act of authority emanating from those who dominate. Thus they say that they have said, this is such or such a thing, they have attached a particular word to an object or a fact and thereby consider themselves to have appropriated it. The women say, so doing the men have bawled, shouted with all their might to reduce you to silence. The women say, the language you speak poisons your glottis tongue palate lips. They say, the language you speak is made up of signs that rightly speaking designate what men have appropriated. Whatever they have not laid hands on, whatever they have not pounced on like many-eyed birds of prey, does not appear in the language you speak. This is apparent precisely in the intervals that your masters have not been able to fill with their words of proprietors and possessors, this can be found in the gaps, in all that which is not a continuation of their discourse, in the zero, the O, the perfect circle that you invent to imprison them and to overthrow them. (pp. 112-14)

In *Les Guérillères*[4] Wittig is claiming not only the right to describe her body — body torn and full of holes — the right to the language of Jeanne Hyvrard, which is essentially still the language of defeat, of victims and exiles allowed their lamentation, but also the right to the real power of words — the appropriation of the world. She wants political speech which transforms not only the individual but the collectivity. She claims the right to have a public identity and therefore to redefine and recreate society. The novel is a call to war; to the assumption of violence, and is a preparation for it: the liberation of women into language.

To achieve this, Wittig reattributes to herself and other women all previous definitions of our society, thereby taking control over the fundamental references upon which our culture stands. Her book is a massive reclaiming of language and literature, a reversal of previous forms, images and usages, and their recreation in a mirror-image society where women are supreme. Gone are the single narrator, unity of tone, precision in space and time, the celebration of the individual, inter-relationship of major and minor characters and the resultant hierarchical forms that shape most male writing. Gone also are all the usual kinds of linear, logical structure and binary opposition attributed to rational "apollonic" thought. *Les Guérillères* is a collection of paragraphs of all kinds of description of the world. Its characteristics are circularity in general, randomness in particular, variety of tone and multiplicity of voices — all feminine. Thus it is the antithesis of the accepted (male) criteria for prose fiction, though it is still built on the previously discussed Garden of Eden elements of naming and sex: language and physical symbols of power.

The book begins with an enormous circle, an O, a zero,[5] and is punctuated at intervals by pages of women's first names, of which the first begins: "What designates them like the Cyclops' eye, their one given name" (p. 15). Thus naming and identity are linked to the circle and the circle to literature and sexuality through the siren's song:

> Somewhere there is a siren ... Sometimes she begins to sing. The women say that of her song nothing is to be heard but a continuous O. That is why this song evokes for them, like everything

that recalls the O, the zero or the circle, the vulval ring. (p. 14)

The vulva is linked to the goddess of the sun:

> The women say that they expose their genitals so that the sun may be reflected therein as in a mirror. They say that they retain its brilliance . . . The glare they shed when they stand still and turn to face one makes the eye turn elsewhere unable to stand the sight. (p. 19)

and to her power which lies in her mirror with which she can destroy the world. The idea of the sun-mirror as weapon to be used in the war against men is then adopted by women also. They use reflections that kill in a reversal of the way in which women have been annihilated for so long by the reflections men have given them of themselves. Their other weapon, called an "ospah" also kills by rays and by its circularity. In this way language, identity, sex and violence are connected throughout the text.

Simultaneously, the "ospah" has a very close counterpart in a delightful game of coloured hoops, and all dances have a circular movement whether peaceful or warlike. The circle become sphere is the shape of the girls' homes; they sleep in spherical egg-sacks, live in floating spheres reminiscent of insect colonies and of the womb. The circle is also the symbol of their action because it is the sign used between warriors to signify both victory and defeat.

The circle dominates the text, giving it structure and meaning; symbol of women's power and sexuality, war and peace, pleasure and violence. It also brings together in the retelling of two of the stories basic to our culture — Adam and Eve, and quest of the Grail — the theme of the double quest of the novel: gain god, gain words, and you gain the world. Eve first (and we notice that Adam has been eliminated totally).

> Sophie Ménade's tale has to do with an orchard planted with trees of every colour. A naked woman walks therein. Her beautiful body is black and shining. Her hair consists of slender mobile snakes which produce music at her every movement. This is the hortative head of hair. It is so called because it communicates by the mouths of its hundred thousand snakes with the woman wearing the headdress. Orpheus, the favourite snake of the woman who walks in the garden, keeps advising her to eat the fruit of the tree in the centre of the garden. The woman tastes the fruit of each tree asking Orpheus the snake how to recognize that which is good.

The answer given is that it sparkles, that merely to look at it rejoices the heart. Or else the answer given is that, as soon as she has eaten the fruit, she will become taller, she will grow, her feet will not leave the ground though her forehead will touch the stars. And he Orpheus and the hundred thousand snakes of her headdress will extend from one side of her face to the other, they will afford her a brilliant crown, her eyes will become as pale as moons, she will acquire knowledge. Then the women besiege Sophie Ménade with questions. Sophie Ménade says that the woman of the orchard will have a clear understanding of the solar myth that all the texts have deliberately obscured. Then they besiege her with questions. Sophie Ménade says, Sun that terrifies and delights/multicoloured iridescent insect you devour yourself in night's memory/blazing genital/the circle is your symbol/you exist from all eternity/you will exist for all eternity. At these words the women begin to dance, stamping the ground with their feet. They begin a round dance, clapping their hands, giving voice to a song from which no coherent phrase emerges. (pp. 52-53)

Thus the sun's symbolic form has been reversed, appropriated to the power of female sexuality and, curiously, has been compared to an insect, bringing us back to the image of the sleeping cells and also to a description of the fighters as insects: "Their faces . . . resemble great insect heads with antennae and stalked eyes" (p. 108) and a suggestion is made by juxtaposition that their army is as multitudinous as an insect army.

Women as insects: ignored or exterminated by the thousand, countless and indestructible, indistinguishable, yet various. This is the image Wittig offers directly: "Their eyes, stuck to a shred of skin, are hidden in their long locks . . . Then each eye, touched, closes its lids, like a firefly going out" (p. 56). And she reinforces the image with the lists of names, frequent use of "they say" and descriptions of giant flowers, marsh water and a game played by the little girls in which they seek out specific perfumes in the dark. Thus the guerillas themselves take shape — innumerable insects whose goddess is the sun to whom they pray:

> I salute you, great Amaterasu, in the name of our mother, in the name of those who are to come. Our kingdom come. May this order be destroyed. May the good and the evil be cast down. (p. 27)

Prayer and scripture are the most powerful forms of language to be won because they form and change the world. Next down the scale comes myth through which the values created by scripture are retold and thus confirmed. Some of the old myths are rejected by the warrior women, the golden fleece for example, others they reformulate. The passage on the Grail legends is the key to the importance of the reclaiming of traditional literature:

> The women say that the feminaries give pride of place to the symbols of the circle, the circumference, the ring, the O, the zero, the sphere. They say that this series of symbols has provided them with a guideline to decipher a collection of legends they have found in the library and which they have called the cycle of the Grail. These are to do with the quests to recover the Grail undertaken by a number of personages. They say it is impossible to mistake the symbolism of the Round Table that dominated their meetings. They say that, at the period when the texts were compiled, the quests for the Grail were singular unique attempts to describe the zero the circle the ring the spherical cup containing the blood. They say that, to judge by what they know about their subsequent history, the quests for the Grail were not successful, that they remained of the nature of a legend. (p. 45)

The legends are re-interpreted in the light of the new belief — and all symbolic foundations of society are revealed as partisan. Here women's blood which was previously taboo has been given a central position in the symbolic network created by the new order. All myths are now open to challenge, lose the implacability of their old authority.

As we move further down the power scale words take on a didactic function rather than a magic one. Myths are followed by the teaching of history on the one hand, fairy tale on the other. As myth, legend and tale come together in *Les Guérillères* let us take fairy tales first. "Sleeping Beauty" is given a female sexual interpretation and comes out like this:

> There is the story of her who fell asleep for one hundred years from having wounded her finger with her spindle, the spindle being cited as the symbol of the clitoris. In connection with this story the women make many jokes about the awkwardness of the one who lacked the priceless guidance of a feminary. They say laughing that she must have been the freak spoken of elsewhere, she who, in place of a little pleasure-greedy tongue, had a poisonous sting. They say they do not understand why she was called the sleeping beauty. (pp. 45-46)

Too far from these girls' experience, it is found ridiculous and put aside. "Snow White and Rose Red" retold, on the other hand, become a different story altogether; the story of the demise of penis envy and woman's loss of fear of phallus power:

> Snow White runs through the forest. Her feet catch in the roots of the trees, which make her trip repeatedly. The women say that the little girls know this story by heart. Rose-Red follows behind her, impelled to cry out while running. Snow-White says she is frightened. Snow-White running says, O my ancestors, I cast myself at your holy knees. Rose-Red laughs. She laughs so much that she falls, that she finally becomes angry. Shrieking with rage, Rose-Red pursues Snow-White with a stick, threatening to knock her down if she does not stop. Snow-White whiter than the silk of her tunic drops down at the foot of a tree. Then Rose-Red red as a peony or else red as a red rose marches furiously to and fro before her, striking the ground with her stick shouting, You haven't got any, you haven't got any, until eventually Snow-White asks, What is it that I have not got? the effect of which is to immobilize Rose-Red saying, Sacred ancestors, you haven't got any. Snow-White says that she has had enough, especially as she is no longer at all frightened and seizing hold of the stick she begins to run in all directions, she is seen striking out with all her might against the tree-trunks, lashing the yielding shrubs, striking the mossy roots. At a certain point she gives a great blow with the stick to Rose-Red asleep at the foot of an oak and resembling a stout root, pink as a pink rose. (pp. 46, 48)

The new tale is also the teaching of woman's right to violence, of little girls' right to use their strength and their bodies in the way boys have always been encouraged to develop. A similar take-over of male prerogatives is shown in the opening paragraph of the book where a game equivalent to who-can-pee-furthest is described.

The fairy tales are all concerned with sexual self-esteem, symbolic status. History on the other hand treats social status. Both the political and personal importance of women are told, sometimes with reference to photographs of women's action in the past — strikes, manifestations, work, sometimes recounted directly in women's words: their description of a shared experience to be passed on to their kind.

> They say, men in their way have adored you like a goddess or else burned you at their stakes or else relegated you to their service in their back-yards . . . They say, they have described you as they described the races they called inferior. (pp. 100 & 102)

And then there is the fiction. All the women in *Les Guérillères* tell stories of one kind or another. Each participates in the description of the world in which she lives, a reversal of the old world and a redefinition of its values. The world is recuperated through the goddesses; the female body and its sex organs in the myths and fairy tales; repression by history; death, violence and pleasure in the other old stories told by the various girls.

> They say, we must disregard all the stories relating to those of them who have been betrayed beaten seized seduced carried off violated and exchanged as vile and precious merchandise . . . *They say that there is no reality before it has been given shape by words rules regulations.* They say that in what concerns them everything has to be remade starting from basic principles. They say that in the first place the vocabulary of every language is to be examined, modified, turned upside down, that every word must be screened. (p. 134. My emphasis)

Here we see the preoccupation with every detail of language that was so evident also in *The Prunes of Cythera*. Language, and thereby power, being in their hands, the women can and must restate and transmit their values. Hence the constant cycle of stories old and new which are a perpetual taking possession of the world. To teach their body to little girls a "feminary" has been written and each copy has blank pages so that each girl can write in her own discoveries and experience. To keep the warriors fighting, war speeches recalling past humiliations are made (see opening quotation). And prisoners are ridiculed with insults that are again the reciprocal of those previously heaped on women:

> When they have a prisoner they strip him and make him run through the streets crying, it is your rod/cane/staff/wand/peg/skewer/staff of lead. Sometimes the subject has a fine body . . . Then they take him by the hand and caress him to make him forget all their bad treatment. (p. 106)

Words that are said, words that are written are public words. Public words are words of power, rituals of possession at every level from prayers to the little girls' games. Naming. The making of symbols. The transmission of values in words. Wittig's women have acquired this power systematically and are living it, or they are struggling for it and are dreaming the power. The world of *Les Guérillères* is reversed, but it is an imprecise and confusing world, recalling utopian science fiction at one moment, ancient Greece at another. Slaves are sometimes slaves but usually they are soldiers and they are always insects, always women.

What is certain in the text is that the powerful metaphors — the sun, blood, sexual organs, a hero's action and death — are brought into the service of female self-esteem, used to support female superiority, to call women to act. So are powerful texts of all kinds. The book begins with little girls at play and builds through the acquisition of a body and a culture to concerted action, action which is always linked to language:

> Then in the sunshine . . . she begins to read an unfolded paper, for example, when the world changes and one day women are capable of seizing power and devoting themselves to the exercise of arms and letters in which they will doubtless soon excell. (p. 135)

Finally the war is fought, the funeral march sung for the dead and we can turn back to the beginning of the book where little girls play boys' games — games of supremacy, games of violence, of skill and of words. Games of power which invest power in those who play them and which are the first and final restatement of the values of the system they are in. The most complex game of all is that played by the book itself. It operates as a mirror reflecting the text of the body and body of the text in the changing light of past, present and future, actual, imaginary and symbolic. The result is a cascade of echoes between the various levels of language and experience until they all combine inextricably to create a new language, a new power base, a new description of the world.

> By the lakeside there is an echo. As they stand there with an open book the chosen passages are re-uttered from the other side by a voice that becomes distant and repeats itself. Lucie Maure cries to the double echo that phrase of *Phénarètes*, I say that that which is is. I say that that which is not also is. When she repeats the phrase several times the double, then triple, voice endlessly superimposes that which is and that which is not. The shadows

brooding over the lake shift and begin to shiver because of the vibrations of the voice. (p. 14)

All that was previously invisible takes its place in the system by means of its opposite: a linguistic reflection reversed.

CHAPTER 8

AND DWELT AMONG US: *L'EUGUELIONNE* (Bersianik)

The Euguélionne (The Bringer of Good Tidings)[1] is also a taking possession of the world by language, following in a direct line from where *Les Guérillères* left off. "They say, moreover, that although laughter is the prerogative of man, they want to learn how to laugh" (p. 124) writes Wittig. Bersianik has learned to laugh and it is through the power of her laughter that she is able to recreate the world her way. Humour, as personal manipulation of language and of the entire symbolic system on which it rests in order to illustrate one's own personal view of things, is one of the ultimate expressions of control, for, as we have seen, the mastery of language is the sign of power. Women, as long as they remain symbols in the system, have no alternative but to remain pawns in a men's game. Bersianik, by making men the target of satire, has challenged a world order then, for she is claiming superiority. And in the practice of humour she overturns that order irrevoccably, for she has proved a control equal to that of men. Her assumption of humour creates her equality and, paradoxically, her assumption of equality creates her humour. She demystifies and deflates the standard, and largely unquestioned, male positions and assertions, simply by translating them from a male to a female perspective. Men are superior, we are taught; yet the apparent difference in stature between the sexes fades away when the roles are reversed and men no longer control the descriptions of events. By Voltairian story-telling Bersianik destroys all the official descriptions we have of ourselves at present, and in so doing reveals the unwarrented, over-weaning sense of their own importance fostered in men by these images of their superiority presented in authoritative statements of male-oriented value systems.

Satire and irony have always been weapons of the strong used against the weak or against (temporarily) more successful equals. As such, it has been male territory for centuries, for women have never been sufficiently at ease in the world to be anything but its victims. Bersianik's accession to humour changes this situation and she does not fail to chide women for having condoned their own humiliation for so long:

> 765. But why are you the first to laugh at their jokes? Why do you pretend to possess their unilateral sense of humour to a very high degree? Is it to obtain their tolerance of your very existence? Is it to apologize for existing? Is it to avoid the punishments that your Men are sure to inflict on you at home, in the office, in the street, in the drawing room; if you are not the accomplices of their insults and their attempts to degrade you? Is it because you have finally become the *opportunists of the species?* or is it because you are still *resigning from the species?* (All translations are my own.)

Misogyny runs deep in our society and in our languages. *The Euguélionne* is a denunciation of its workings and its results. To this end the novel is an analysis of the dominant discourses which reinforce each other in the support of men and the repression of women, and which are responsible for the major symbolic networks of our language: Christianity and psychology.

The novel is in three parts, each restating the theme— the inequality of man and woman — in one of the linguistic modes by which we normally have the world told to us: allegory, description/example, explanation. Or, to be more precise, given the power of *The Euguélionne*, in the modes of scripture: parable, gospel and sermon. (The book is divided into chapter and verse and numbered accordingly.)

Like Wittig, Bersianik begins by reclaiming the most powerful description of the world: The Bible. The Euguélionne arrives on earth and, as in the beginning was the word and the word was with god, she gives a press conference immediately, in which she states her objective: "Me," said the Euguélionne, "I'm looking for my positive planet." All come away with a different impression of her, according to their background and attitude: Venus de Milo, Victory of Samothrace, Statue of Liberty. One Australian writes down and elaborates his description and the goddess comes into being officially: and the word god!

Part of a female trinity, a Divine Triangle made up of Mother, Daughter and Supreme Brain, the Euguélionne is provided with a long geneology running from the Goddess Wondjina and Eve, whom she created as mother of all things, through Mary Magdalene who begat Salomé who begat the Virgin Mary who begat Phaedra, down to Virginia Woolf who begat Simone de Beauvoir who begat Betty Friedan who begat Kate Millett who begat La Nopaline who begat the Euguélionne in a properly complicated Virgin Birth:

The Emasculate Conception.
152. The Euguélionne's conception was virginal, the Australian orator who seemed better documented on the question than anyone else, continued on the air-waves.

The Euguéllionne's real father remained chaste even if he was half responsible for the Euguélionne's conception. The other half being the work, not of La Nopaline but of Wondjina's Supreme Brain. La Nopaline is only the putative mother of the Euguélionne, even though, as we have seen, she is of royal descent.
153. And this is how the Euguélionne was engendered: La Nopaline her mother was betrothed to Le Nopal. Now, before they had lived together, Le Nopal, like a seahorse, found that he was the carrier of a divine ovule which fertilized itself unbeknown to him, with his own gamete.

All this came to pass as the messenger of the Most High Wondjina, Archangel Evangeline, had announced to him.

At this annunciation Le Nopal had replied: "I am the servant of the Most High Wondjina, be it done according to her holy Will."
154. That ovule came then from the Supreme Brain and the junction of the two cells constituting the Divine Egg was accomplished without impurity, without fornication.
155. When La Nopaline, who was an honest young girl, learned that her future husband was an unmarried-father she did not want to denounce him publicly (because the inevitable prestation of the Social Well-Being would have betrayed his situation and besmirched his reputation), nor did she make him have an abortion!

After cogitating on the problem for several days — she had to be quick, the pregnancy was advancing — she decided to repudiate the guilty man quietly.
156. She was thinking about this when the Extra-Terrestrial messenger of the Most High Wondjina, Archangel Evangeline appeared to her in a dream and said: "La Nopaline, daughter of Bethsheba, do not be afraid to cohabit with Le Nopal, your future husband. For what has been engendered on him comes from the Supreme Brain . . ."

In this manner an antipodean theologian creates the reverse order from the same matter as the first one. But, before the Euguélionne's birth is told, the testament of the previous order is established by a series of parable-reports, the first of which shows discrimination created by language. It concerns the Euguélionne's native planet where it seems that the inhabitants are of two kinds: females called "Pédaleuses" and males called "Législateurs." Each is labelled on the forehead at birth, females with the words NIGRA SUM SED FORMOSA ("Black I am but beautiful" from the Song of Songs), males with DURA LEX SED LEX (the law is hard but it is the law), and each must play the inscribed role. There is a slippage in the inscriptions whenever they are read by somebody else, because from the outside they are seen backwards, thus becoming FORMOSA SUM SED NIGRA and LEX SED DURA LEX. Hence woman is pushed further into her negritude while man becomes more intractible in his dominance by the effect of the instability of language.

The second parable shows woman as universal uterus. A constantly pregnant woman is described as a haunted house out of which an unending stream of children are pulled on strings: boy children as soldiers, girls as domestic slaves. Their future is decided, their roles distributed. The woman, too, is manipulated by strings.

The third is Alice-come-back-from-Wonderland's rejection of her role as Victorian child trapped in an everlasting snare of language, injustice, repression and deliberate confusion. The original story is retold with reversals and commentary. (1) Playing cards and people: "législateurs" are as varied as the faces of the cards, "pédaleuses" as undifferentiated as the backs and as unimportant in the active part of the game. (2) Words and people: "Législateurs" are verbs, "pédaleuses" adjectives. (3) Men only walk upright when wearing crowns, otherwise they are bent and abject. (4) The Mad Hatter's tea party and decision-making bodies — no room for women. (5) Elsie, Lacie and Tilly living in a treacle well and why they do not create great works of art. (6) Alice trying to remember her name is a "pédaleuse" in search of an identity. (7) It is neither possible to sweep all the sand off a beach nor all the dust away. (8) The ticket collector wants to send Alice home because she is too delicate to travel. Failing this she must be confused until she loses her way. (9) Alice learns she must run twice as fast as the "législateurs" to get to the same spot otherwise she will be disqualified even if she ran faster than they did. Alice concludes that the rules should be changed. (10) The Duchess throws pots and the baby. According to the Cheshire Cat the baby can become either a "cochon" (pig) or a "torchon" (dish towel). (11) The Griffon told Alice about the man and woman each married to an octopus who sucked them dry.

The fourth story is that of the human race: "Mascles" and "Fems"; how the "Mascles" came to think themselves superior because they each had a Marechal's bâton and "Fems" did not. Therefore "Fems" must have been demoted for some wrong and had their bâtons taken away — hence they must be treated as if inferior and in disgrace, and put aside from everything important except reproduction.

Thus the old testament lore of the growth of symbolic male dominance by the law and the phallus, and a parallel reduction of female scope into appearance and incoherent agitation is laid out. It only remains for the story of Adam and Eve to be told and the time will be ripe for the Eugélionne's birth.

In the beginning Adam was bored so he began to have evil thoughts:

113. "What," he said to himself aloud, peering at his 'organ.' "Must it be that this organ which should be so proud, will be called upon to perform vulgar functions only? . . . but where, where is the Nothingness to compensate its Being to be found?" As we can see, Adam had no lack of the gracious modesty later characteristic of his sex . . .

115. First, as soon as he saw Eve, father-mother Adam was struck by her strange appearance. On the upper part of her body she had two erect things which pointed at him unfalteringly. But having lowered his eyes . . . Eve had no organ! What a catastrophe! *Adam had given birth to a handicapped child! . . .*

This Nothingness awful, terrifying as it was was that to which he aspired . . .

117. Eve gazed at him incredulously.

"It's not possible! The world is upside down! My father-mother is maimed! First he has no breasts. And then I think he is in the process of losing his vulva and all that goes with it . . . *Please Jahweh may I never be done up like that . . ."*

119. "You'd like something like that, hey?" he said . . . "Me, have something like that!" cried Eve more surprised than offended by Adam's mistake, mistake that was perpetuated for centuries, alas. "What a funny idea! Without wishing to vex, I find it rather disgusting, if you really want to know. It's as if you asked me something like 'would you like to be crippled or nuts?' Well, I mean . . . [sic]"

Eve has both pride in her body and a certain mastery of language by which to defend her interests. She finds herself equal if not superior and is impervious to suggestions of penis envy. Adam produces his first erection in imitation and envy of her breasts. The story from which all theory of female inferiority stems in our culture has been reclaimed and the Euguélionne now has a base in scripture from which to preach the re-instatement of women in society. The saviour has come to take the load of guilt and shame from their shoulders. In the manner of her predecessor she does it by the appropriation of language in her teaching and by the symbolic value of her death.

As the Euguélionne's farewell speech draws to a close in a demand for justice and equality, a Judas-woman throws a stone and a platoon of soldiers shoot the Euguélionne, who shatters into a thousand pieces which stay suspended in the air. Like the women Bersianik described before, she is a man's target, but the fragmented Euguélionne reassembles:

> 1349. The Euguélionne then reappeared: all her pieces fit back together as in a moving puzzle, filmed at accelerated speed or as in a film of destruction played backwards.

Her death is a denial of the time when women were destroyed by men. She is the sign of the new order of indestructibility of women, an order where women believe in their lives and have control over them — no more fragmentation, no longer victim, no longer "dead."

> 1350. I told you I shouldn't die, said the Euguélionne. Too many things to do. Overloaded programme. No time to croak. I'm leaving.

The old testament is followed by the gospel: deflated, retold, reclaimed. Just as in *Les Guérillères* the scriptures are taken over first because of the authority they embody, and then comes the turn of all public langauge by which the world is constantly reaffirmed: literature, ceremonial, law, publicity. The word having become feminine in the first part of the novel, Bersianik explores woman's relationship to language in everyday life in Part II.

First we see woman's private life told in a latter day anti-fairy tale. The Euguélionne helps Omicronne-Cinderella to come into her own, not by marriage to her prince but rather by escape from it. Prince Charming is Alfred Omega, whose name explains his attitude and position as clearly as does the prince's. He thinks he is the beginning and end of all things, and also/because he is a master of language who has the right to speak for and about everybody — especially his princess.

> 244. Mr. Alfred Omega is a relatively young university professor.

He also has his moments as a literary critic. Mr. Omega even directs a specialized journal that he considers very important. Mr. Omega is very active . . .

Mr. Omega has given his respectable name to little Omicronne. Mr. Omega has even given his respected name to two or three children. Mr. Omega is very generous.

245. . . . "Professorial lectures are finished, out of date, no one gives them any more," he says in a very professorial tone.

"That's it," I said to myself. "That's the word. Mr. Omega uses professorial language. He, himself, is a Master. Mr. Omega talks like a master. He knows what he is saying."

The secret of power is revealed in the logic of the Euguélionne's description: Omega has learned to employ a certain tone of voice from which comes a certain language. Because of this language it is assumed that he is as important as he sounds, and therefore he is listened to with respect. His power is a pure function of his idea of himself. Spoken self-importance becomes real, born of words. The reverse is also true. Bersianik's deflation of M. Omega is a reflection of Omega's treatment of Omicronne. He describes her, and by his words he creates her in a certain context and evaluates her at the same time. An integral part of the way he recounts her is by systematic devaluation of her accomplishments; she is an excellent artist about whose work her husband says: "247. 'That? That's nothing. Pay no attention. My wife amuses herself that way in her spare time.' "

His words are humiliating, and are the exact reverse of the treatment he accords his own occupations, as we have seen. He undermines Omicronne while building himself up. The process is continued in his treatment of her body which he fragments and depersonalizes: "249. 'Look at this pretty behind, isn't it tempting?' " She is his possession.

The princess, Omicronne, slaves in the kitchen and weeps into the washing-up water until the Euguélionne fairy godmother teaches her what to do:

> 253. You can choose the best part too. If you are a person
> Omicronne, leave your dish-towel there and follow me.

Meanwhile, Epsilonne, Omicronne's sister, plays the step-mother role by supporting the men in their misogynic behaviour. She is a psychologist, and throughout the novel refuses to recognize women's problems or to give women any support at all. She speaks male language, has been accepted into male society, lives by their code and spends her professional life inculcating it into other women.

Omicronne walks out on them all, fitting her action to her definition of herself as a person, and sets out to find her identity — her name, the one she had before she became Mrs. Alfred Omega. This is the one word that belongs to her by right, and is the key to all the others. During her search she goes to a government supported theatre school to learn to speak in public. She finds herself in the same old situation in which women are objectified and humiliated as the normal course of affairs: the scene is a beer commercial.

> 398. On each step, he strokes a chin, a cheek, a breast . . . and stroking here and there as he goes, he sings . . .
>   Yes I love blonds,
>   Yes I love redheads . . .
>   But she I like best
>   Is Zigande-et-une* beer.
> (*A deformation of "cinquante-et-un" — 51.)

Then Omicronne reverses the roles. In her turn she takes the same words and uses them to reduce men's self-esteem by treating them as fragmentary bits of anatomy, toys to play with:

> 401/2. Omicronne goes from one to the other, caressing this one . . . pulling a moustache or mop of hair . . . she sings
>   I like smooth men
>   I like beardless ones . . .
>   But he I prefer is a gin n' tonic, or rather no, it's a stiff and virile scotch-on-the-rocks.

The result is total outrage. A taboo has been infringed; chastisement is swift and public. The offending female must be obliged to avow her inferiority — power of words again — in a sacramental confession.

> 403. "It's a passage from *The Hostage* by Paul Claudel" said the leader . . . "We're going to read you a short scene. The priest asks the heroine to sacrifice herself . . . Sygne, the heroine, replies: *Oh who am I, poor girl, to compare myself to the male of my race!* . . . Go on, its your turn, Omicronne, give me my cue . . ."
> "Go on, go on," says the leader . . . "Oh who am I, poor girl . . . .etc.[sic] You only have to read it, it's not difficult."
> But Omicronne says not a word.
> So the leader loses his temper.

"You shall say the line immediately."
"I shall not say it," says Omicronne calmly. "It's abject."
(My emphasis)

(Included in the scene we also get a side comment on the way literature supports the male-dominated *status quo*.) When Omicronne both refuses to submit and re-affirms her right to criticize men: "404. 'Ah, who are you, poor male, to believe yourself incomparable!' " she is booed off the stage. She has not yet realized that if she is taught to speak in public by a school belonging to the establishment she will be taught to play time-consecrated, male-oriented roles.

Thus in private and in public men undermine women constantly by objectification of their bodies, a general dehumanization produced by the abject roles they are given in society, and a total veto on the right to self-expression in language. The pivot of this system is marriage, and Bersianik reveals all its inherent abuse by putting a parody of the ceremony in the heart of the novel as a play which the Euguélionne and her friends see. Its traditional, authority-ridden prose translated into specifics, its underlying assumptions stated bluntly, it stands revealed as a simple slave-trade transaction.

The play as an affirmation of society to itself; theatre as ritual; ceremony as male entertainment; the marriage ceremony is the point at which religious and civil phallocratism come together in a theatrical proof of the power of the verbal agreement, the giving of one's word, the sacred weight invested by tradition in the pact, for what else holds women in a state of servitude but the Word and its solemn public statement? The male side of the agreement is clear and simple: father gives his daughter to another male who will keep her in his turn in exchange for her obedience and for the purpose stated at the beginning of the play — that he may lay all the trivial things of life upon her. She is a consumable and disposible commodity in a male market. A permanent "au pair" girl, as the Euguélionne remarks elsewhere.

The female side of the arrangement has never been stated. This Bersianik does in a cascade of words which are provided with a glossary in the novel for the audience, who is not expected to be familiar with them. Female-slave words with which "they will be able to make sentences if they want to express some *Housewives' Exploits*," remarks the programme; "It's a very simple and extremely amusing game" — patronizing again. Thereupon follows a 37 paragraph inventory of household jobs (!) of which I quote one or two that touch on the major themes I have been discussing:

447. — Order, may your kingdom come. Watchword: Order every-

where! In Papers. In Pockets. In Linen. In Corners. In Nooks. In Depths. On the Stairs. Under the Stairs. In the Condiments. In the food. In cupboards. In ashtrays. In the bottoms of cups where the future is written. Order in the ashes of Others. *The Great Vacuum Cleaner.*
Suppliers. The telephones. The plumber . . . The budget. The Correspondence. *Tax returns. Sexual relations (returns).* Seventh heaven! Love of the Other. The specks on the ceiling.
Monthly blood. Menstrual blood. Disgusting blood. *Women's dirty blood.* The absent Koitus [sic]. Kotex. Tampax. *Shameful sickness.* No Koitus for those who have been bled dry. Contraception. The miraculous pill. Above all think to take the pill. Stop the pill: nerves in a knot. Have an IUD put in. Have the IUD taken out: bleeding womb. Hail to you guinea-pig womb. Abortion: urgent. Do it cleanly. Find a way. Stop. The law wants it to be dirty. Law wants blood. *Uterine blood belongs to the state.* Stop. The corner butcher. Wants to be paid in cash. Find money. Signed: Domestic Womb.
PRAISE of dirty hands. Analstage.
PRAISE of white hands in black water. *Analysstage.* Red and black.
NOBILITY intrinsically inherent in the act of cleaning toilet bowls. *Analysttage.* (My emphasis)

Concerned with only the dirt left by others and others' vision of herself as dirty by her very nature, woman is being driven crazy to the point of thinking of psychoanalysis, which will only drive her more deeply into servitude and a sense of her own inferiority, as we know from watching Dr. Phipsi and Epsilonne.

This is the bride's very own vocabulary, and one which is not spoken, not even here: it is a programme note. The way in which these activities are translated into publically acceptable speech is illustrated by the poem written and recited by the bride's mother and entitled "You will be a Real Woman, my Daughter, or the Ten Commandments of the Married Woman." It begins like this:

> 464. If you consecrate your life to the *service* of your husband and your children who will pay it back one hundred fold, the first by keeping you, the second by growing in wisdom and cries under your eyes and in your ear . . .

and continues via a veto on taking man's place in the work market or any other place of power or administration, on imitating man in any way, exhortation to smile and never make a man feel guilty no matter what he does, etc., to the final injunction:

> 464. If you find your love torn, mend it or throw it in the nettles *as long as you keep your place in the home** YOU WILL BE A TRUE WOMAN MY DAUGHTER. (*My emphasis)

Therefore a Real Woman is a servant struggling to deep her job.

In Bersianik's ceremony all the underlying values of marriage are made visible and the humiliation involved made clear:

> 459. The young bride who was coming forward *on her father's arm*, radiant, dainty, gown immaculate . . . [an Officiant] was approaching holding . . . a solid gold tray that he presented to the future wife pronouncing, in the purest tradition of civil and religious weddings, these solemn words, marked by the seriousness of the moment:
> "Here is your shit. Here is the shit of your husband* and here is that of your future children. It is to you and you only that I entrust these sublime materials for only you can rid your home of it *with elegance* . . .
> The future wife received this symbolic offering with veneration and love. (*These two sentences are in English in the text. My emphasis)

The idealized sentiments covering the silence concerning woman's real situation are swept away in this new description. Once told, the situation exists and the taboo on women's language has been broken.

The play continues with a further image of the female condition, and one which is reminiscent of a fairy tale again: a woman is chained into a cell with glass walls and insults are chanted around her. She is in a glass coffin. The image recurs later in the novel in a piece of political, domestic and psychological counterpoint which is worth quoting at length.

> 509. One day, the Euguélionne said, we were invited to the house of some very rich, very snobbish people of good position, a young couple with a baby several months old . . .
> 510. Omicronne drew our attention to a funeral parlour window where coffins were on display. It looked as though some of them

were made of glass and even . . . occupied. [sic]

511 We see a child lying on its side in a glass coffin . . . Other skeletic corpses of both sexes and various ages are "on show" in the coffins in the window. We don't understand how this is possible and why the municipal authorities allow such a macabre exhibition. The passers-by don't seem to be affected by the sight. They stop in front of the window and discuss the solidity of the coffins and their luxurious padding . . .

513. We go along a long, wide, well-lit corridor. Near the middle of this corridor, all three of us get a violent shock. See in the wall about halfway between the floor and the ceiling there is a sort of narrow window that's not very long. The glass is a smooth continuation of the wall.

And in this glass cage we see the baby of the house crawling around surrounded by toys. It looks quite alive . . . [sic] We assume that prevision has been made for changing the air . . . [sic] The window is such that one can watch the child without having to stoop or stretch: it really is at average adult eye-level.

Our young hosts run to meet us. They are determined to talk to every one of their guests themselves about the comforts of this magnificent, transparent little room, the *nec plus ultra* of modern child care. They are obviously delighted with what they consider the ideal solution of the problem of Baby's arrival. Indeed it has christened its new "nest" this very day.

514. "You understand," says the young mother, *"It's a little girl! We thought she should have maximum protection!*

"This way," the 'happy father' explains to us, "our dear little one is isolated enough from the rest of the household to be able to play or sleep in peace, *without being 'disturbed.'* And we can watch her games without being inconvenienced. *The fairly restricted space she has has been calculated with the aim of making her feel secure: she should feel surrounded, enveloped!* Isn't it a fantastic invention! But, better yet:this marvellous nursery has an ingenious device which raises the ceiling at the rate the child grows, *so that she will never be traumatised at seeing herself grow* . . . [sic] *phenomenon that we cannot prevent, alas!* Besides, don't you find that this ultra-modern installation could be mistaken for a giant television screen? *In this way it has the added merit of offering our guests a charming spectacle* when they go through here on their way to the drawing rooms. This way ladies, we are almost . . ."

515. We soon learn that this social gathering . . . has been organized at these people's home under the auspices of a *house-wifery school for young ladies.*

Exil tells the young hostess that in our day it's shameful to go on teaching housewifery to girls without teaching it to boys as well as later they will need it just as much as girls.

"You do not realize, Madame, how pejorative the term 'housewife' is in our society, how it is unconsciously scorned by everybody, even the best of us."

To support what she is saying, Exil opens a newspaper she has taken out of her bag and starts searching for an article. It's a leftist weekly and the article she finds is signed by an ardent defender of the rights of the oppressed.

"Listen to the conclusion of this article:
The incompetent men who govern us take refuge in a policy of immobility and behave like cowmen or housewives. After that do you dare to say that there is not such thing as a *stupid job?*
516. The young woman is astounded. She was certainly not expecting that kind of outburst from one of her guests. And that impious newspaper, that systematically contentious paper! Spread out in her drawing room! What cheek! . . . Fortunately the announcement of a speech creates a diversion.

It will be given by the headmistress of the domestic science school for young ladies, a nun in civilian clothes . . .
517. "You know, 'home economics' have their place in our society today as yesterday. Woman is always required to play her woman's role. Examples come from on high. Hasn't Princess Anne of England just *sworn to obey* her new husband in front of millions of telespectators and the Archbishop of Canterbury? Protestant though he may be he is still one of the venerable partiarchs whom Christians must obey!"

Finally the Sister-headmistress concludes her homily in terms that Exil and Omicronne consider revolting:

"And you know that young husbands today, just like those in the past, demand that their wives have a high level of domestic skill. Young girls should know this and be ready to satisfy Men on this point at least by the time they are nineteen!"

These words trigger prolonged applause.

As soon as all is silent again, Exil takes the nun to task publically.

518. "Nineteen! Nineteen you say! Aren't you ashamed? Aren't you ashamed to go on forming slaves in the space-rocket age!" . . .
519. . . . Without appearing ruffled, the young husband comes and politely asks Exil to leave.
520. When we go back past the window, we see the baby collapsed and lying on its back, its eyes wide open, staring. However carefully we look, we can see no sign of breathing in its little chest nor between its half-open lips. The same fear seizes us. Omicronne looks at us: "Is she asleep or is she . . ." [sic]
She does not dare say out loud what we are all thinking quietly . . . [sic]
We flee from this house, terrorized. (*My emphasis)

First we see the dead as consumer products in "jars" in a shop window. They are obviously considered a natural part of society. Next we see a specific repression-murder in action. A girl-child is restricted in her activities from birth; she is prevented from realizing her own growth, even from having any but the vaguest notions that such a thing as development exists. She is constantly on display — "une belle image" — and in a Skinner box for the ultimate in psychological control and conditioning.

The link between this imprisoned childhood and life in a school of home economics is an easy one to make. Both are preparation for a life of domestic service after a wedding as a princess. The Euguélionne dots the I's and crosses the T's for us on this point with her reference here to Princess Anne, and follows it up elsewhere with her comment on lovesongs: that every troubador has a dedicated little woman at home doing the dirty work necessary to maintain the life of universal love and openness about which he sings. Songs: yet another way in which male dominance is affirmed and woman's condition mystified by language.

Women are conditioned into playing certain kinds of roles by the constant shaping of their context, a shaping which is intended to maintain male supremacy and maximise women's confusion. The Euguélionne explains the situation in a way that links the parables she told in the beginning with the meaning of the beer commercial episode and the wedding play. All is theatre: the parts are distributed at birth and the play is already written.

852. "BIRTH," said Euguélionne, "is the same for a girl as for a boy . . ."
853. But the play begins at that moment. And that's where the difference starts.

854. They notice that the boy has ten extremely prehensile fingers and say enthusiastically: "That one is going to take over the world!" And all his entourage help him put his little prehensile fingers on the world even before he's opened his eyes.

They also notice with consternation that the girl has ten extremely prehensile little fingers too and they say in terror, "If we're not careful that one is going to want to take over the world!" Then they catch her on the wing and lock her into a vicious circle.

And her extremely prehensile little fingers grasp the void of this vicious circle even before she's opened her eyes.

This vicious circle can be expressed as follows: "She must not take over the world because she's a girl; she's a girl because she cannot take over the world."

Thus it is that she starts going round and round all her life, that will be her apprenticeship. And as she grows older and for some inexplicable reason revolts more often, they complain: "Girls are so complicated!"

A girls's power of understanding is deliberately handicapped. Not only that, but she is given less from which to learn, and what she is given is confusing in the message it relays about her identity and role. No wonder she cannot express herself in language. Look at this:

> 714. "Just like Man," said the Euguélionne, "the French language has capitalized the species to the profit of Men . . .
> 717. . . . the language is [so] miserly towards women, not in qualifying them — no holds barred there! — but in substantifying them. The word 'femme' [woman] is a master key together with 'fille' [girl] which is supposed to indicate consanguinity.
> I propose to give you a little monologue in which the word 'fille' designates successively sex, consanguinity, virginity, spinsterhood/celibacy and prostitution:
> At home we were three children: two boys and a girl [fille]. I had two: a son and a daughter [fille]. Look at me in this photo, it dates from the time when I was still unmarried/a virgin [fille in both cases] . . . [sic] But I never married, I remained a spinster [fille]. And now look what I've become: I'm a prostitute ['fille'] now!"
> 718. . . . She said, we could establish a little comparative chart

of these strange semantics...

Man –	HOMME – HUMANITE –	Humanity
man–	homme...femme	–woman
husband–	mari...femme	–wife
male–	mâle...femelle	–female
son–	fils...fille	–daughter
boy–	garçon...fille	–girl
	fille	–prostitute
masculine–	masculin...féminin	–feminine
virile –	viril...féminin	–feminine
virility–	virilité...féminité	–femininity
masculinity–	masculinité...féminité	–femininity

"You see, gentlemen," said the Euguélionne, "you see why women are dumb... As if they had their tongues cut out."

This constant shift in meaning between the approbatory and the pejorative in words defining women is at the root of the princess-witch, idealized and rejected view women have of themselves. And this division, repeated in the fragmentation of their bodies in description, and the split between body and accomplishment, is what keeps them in a state of inferiority. Also, all words describing women who talk are negative in implication. Part II of *The Euguélionne* ends with an example of this taken from a school text.

Thus women are repressed by words, by the male authority invested in language as it takes expression at every level of society, personal, public, official or sacred.

The Euguélionne is and preaches a new world in which there is a Female Word also, a world in which women have access to the sacerdoce, to the elaboration of theories and the making of symbols which uphold and transmit their values. The formulae from which the world is calculated must be revised to read:

1145. In woman:	feminine pole	– active and positive
	masculine pole	– passive and negative
In man:	masculine pole	– active and positive
	feminine pole	– passive and negative

Before this can be achieved, however, the exclusive rule of male monotheism must be challenged. Omicronne tried and failed because when she reversed the roles in the beer commercial she kept and tried to use the original language. This was not possible. The system cannot be overthrown from inside by one if its symbols trying to change its function. Alice explained that in her story about verbs and adjectives. As we saw in Bersianik's description of the wedding, the power language is challenged best when it is translated into another idiom which is free of all the signs of authority invested in the first.

The phallocratic scripture, based on the law Ψ (psi) is preached by St. Siegfried (Freud):

> 634. The Phallus is the Fundamental Value of every human individual . . . It is the *Nec Plus Ultra* of the human condition, it is the Essential Norm of the Human Being, it is his condition *sine qua non*. No salvation except by the Phallus! Consider it well my privileged brothers, my poor deprived sisters.

All women's attitudes, actions and language are therefore intepreted according to the tables of the law:

> 640. Dear Madam, it is obvious that you are suffering from your Specific Lack and that you are manifesting a strong *penis envy*, which is quite normal, however, in persons of your sex.

The challenge to this, the dominant, nay only, religion, comes from a little girl who has escaped conditioning by having received an "underground" education. Let us watch the match, Zazie v. Freud.

> 641. "Penis envy my ass," shouted a cheeky little voice.
> "Who said that?" inquired St. Siegfried, untroubled.
> "Me," said a sharp-looking little girl sitting astride a branch.
> "What's your name?" said the Master.
> "Me, I'm called Zazie, and you?"
> "Let's not talk about me. Tell me Zazie, where did you go to school?"
> "In the subway like everybody else! And you?"
> "Let's not talk about me" said St. Siegfried. "So, my little Zazie, you don't want a little thing your brother owns that you, alas, don't have?"
> "What is it exactly you want to talk about?" said Zazie, "Would it be Jojo's dong? Gee, you're a funny 'un. Still I'll tell you in confidence: I'd much rather have tits like mummy than a dong.

They'd be more useful for catching fellas."

"But don't you think Jojo's little tap is useful?"

642. "Tap my ass," said Zazie, "I can pee without that, so can't see why I should have plumbing as well. What would I do with it? And then, Mister, still between ourselves, I've got things my little brother hasn't got. Believe it or not, when he puts his fingers up his nose, I'm not going around wishing I had his little tap, as you call it, because, Mister, I can put my fingers somewhere but it isn't up my nose, that I can guarantee. I even hide my marbles in that 'somewhere'! Still between ourselves isn't it? If y'ever want a hiding place like that too, all I can tell you is that it's really super!"

Laugher broke out everywhere. But St. Siegfried wasn't convinced and wanted to lead the child on to make a full confession.

"You mean, little Zazie, that you have never, *never* wanted to own your little brother's little thing?"

"I do sometimes," said the child nostagically.

"There! You see," said the Master, "and when would that be?"

643. "It's always when my mother makes me wash the dishes, that I envy him that way. 'Cos him, he's always on holiday. Do you think that's fair?"

Zazie, like Eve before her, reclaims the honour of her breasts, refuses all suggestion of penis envy and reasserts the fundamental injustice of the way things are. In Zazi's world the Phallus does not exist. She recognizes the human sized penis on her lucky brother only, considers its real function, and proclaims herself equal.

Thus the religion that has been built up around the phallus, phallus as power and phallus as symbol, having been deprived of its ceremonial text, is stripped of its authority. Priests and sectarians alike can no longer claim superiority because they are numbered amongst its worshippers. The taboo is broken. The Word is no longer sacred, and in female language undergoes an immediate transformation:

648. Wassa Peripaphillobus Mister? Z'it some sort of overhead subway?

You don't say a Parapaphillusse . . . it's a Papapouphallusse.

and so on, until, reduced by the word games of the delighted little girls, the Phallus takes form thus:

> 649. It's Jesus Christ's   (pronounced Jesus Chree)
> Little wee-wee
> That's not so thick
> As a matchstick
> That doesn't stop him
> Going to pee
> Long live the wee-wee
> Of Jesus Christ
> Good Lord! ("Hostie" means the Host. I have given the exclamatory English equivalent.)

Man having been reduced to size linguistically at the highest level of authority: scripture, the time is ripe for the Euguélionne to state her precepts for revolution. Part III of the novel thus restates the themes of the first two in the two contrasting sermon sequences. St. Siegfried preaches overtly the law depicted in the Euguélionne's parables. Next the Euguélionne will deal directly with the social inequalities observed in Part II. There follows an analysis of misogyny and the distortions of reality it has produced. Rooted in language and physical sex differences, its results are multiple and always to the detriment of women.

The Euguélionne calls on women to claim their bodies, their language and with them their rights. She states her oppostion to the phallocentric cult directly:

> 1280. It's very simple, St. Siegfried, they want their part of the cake!
> They want their fair share of your Cake of Life that you and your equals have always scoffed totally, leaving only crumbs for women.
> . . .
> 1285. And, above all, St. Siegfried, don't pray for them any longer! They've told me they've had enough of the Capitalists of the Species who pray for them and live in their stead.

Immediately after her death, her disciples, acting on her advice, create their own value system with its all-powerful symbol. In opposition to the elitist, exclusive Phallus, they offer the all-inclusive, egalitarian religion of the

Hole. The last taboo has been broken as the most insulted, invisible and desired part of insulted, invisible and desired woman is named, and in its naming reversed. What has been vilified becomes sacred, the centre of the new language, the new world:

> 1383. Woman, my sister, man my brother, may your sign no longer be either the cross or the law, but rather *the tree of holes.*
> *In the Name of the welcoming Hole, and the penetrating Hole and the evacuating Hole, Amen.*

And so Bersianik turns the world inside out in the manner of Voltaire. The strength of *The Euguélionne* lies in its direct application of its own advice: "Resisting is good . . . transgressing is better" (v. 1019). The novel challenges all taboos; it satirizes all that has been considered sacrosanct on the grounds that on such myth is mythological power built; it talks openly about all that has been forbidden because with secrecy comes repression, with silence comes weakness and invisibility. The gasp of shock, chuckle of satisfaction and burst of laughter follow each other in quick succession as Bersianik takes over the world with the weapon of ridicule.

" 'What do I want?' said the Euguélionne. 'EVERYTHING! I WANT EVERYTHING!' " (v. 12) Men bear the brunt of her attack as most of the things she wants are in their possession. Their foibles are laughed at, their weaknesses criticized, their superiorities undermined, their power challenged and frequently defeated, their pretentions mocked. They share for the first time the usual daily experience of all women. A description of themselves is provided for them and they become objects for exchange. Looking in the mirror they see themselves frozen in attitudes in which others see them all the time.

Women are not treated any more gently, however. Stripped of the traditional idealizations that envelop the roles of bride, wife, and mother, they see themselves without paint as abject slaves, *arriviste* or down-trodden, condoning by their responses the petty dictatorship of every male.

Bersianik's writing has the same attributes as the Euguélionne's eyes: it can see everything as though it were under a microscope, and can see through it as well. One eye is sad and one is gay: thus we are aware of both the injustice and ridiculousness of every situation. New eyes, new perception, new reflection. It is an unusual and sobering experience for men to see themselves described by someone other than another man, for the description to be a mockery of their view of themselves, and for them to be expected to laugh with those who are undermining their dignity and self-esteem. It is a new and stimulating experience for women to laugh at themselves together with one of their own kind and to laugh at others from a position of strength. The result is true equality. And herein lies what is revolutionary in *The Euguélionne*. Satire is not new; what is new is that it is no longer exclusive male territory.

The Euguélionne herself (like the Phallus for men) is set up as a symbol to which women should aspire; a symbol which is the absolute antithesis of the dead princess from whom we started. She is active, articulate and, above all, able to put herself back together whenever men reduce her to fragments in an attempt to kill her — a woman who will not die. Curiously, however, these two embodiments of the myth of women's weakness and the myth of women's power have one very important thing in common: each is perfect and fits perfectly into the best of all possible worlds. (Remember the dead women floating around the boat taking Upsilong and Alfred Omega to the Isle of Cythera?) It just depends on whose world it is, doesn't it?

CHAPTER 9

A FAIRY TALE CONCLUSION:
"A BAD READING" (Delaunay)

With *The Euguélionne* we have been taken far beyond the scope of the other novels discussed in this book. Most of the others describe individuals, each isolated in her own situation, dealing with it as best she can, while at the same time she is cut off from all other women, a symbol of their general and shared condition. Only Beauvoir, amongst the early novelists, gives some social perspective, some sense of general truth to the story she tells, allowing Laurence the perspicacity to recognize her problems in other lives, if not to find any acceptable solution there. The rest are chronicles of personal exile.

Hébert, Beauvoir, Duras and Blais, all depict women damaged by the context within which they must live. Diminished, fragmented by the demands of society and their menfolk, they struggle to achieve some satisfactory degree of unification of their feelings and behaviour which have been divided by an alien system of which they are the victims.

Nor, except perhaps in *Les Belles Images,* does the reader sense any support or even sympathy for the characters. Indeed, the very style of writing emphasises the isolation of each of the women by showing a detachment of author for her heroine. At all levels, patriarchal language control seems to be effective.

This changes when we come to the writing of Hyvard and Wittig. They are involved with their characters, striving to overcome the division caused by the presentation of woman as object/other, and to achieve the presentation of each woman as an active, feeling subject using her own language. Together with their heroines, Hyvard and Wittig assume the alienation that has been imposed upon them. Hyvard's heroine is mad, her madness the sign to herself and to all around her of her difference, of the fact that she has her own values by which she lives. She is an "acceptable" heroine turned inside out. A cracked image of what a woman is expected to look like, but a true reflection of herself. In her madness she is whole.

What Hyvard does for the individual, Wittig does for society. She turns it around and produces a mirror image of the male-dominated, phallocratic system — a society of Amazons concerned with the importance of woman's multiplicity and her accession to violence.

The assumption of otherness in a world that treats women as "others" is a step in the right direction certainly, but, rightway up or upside down, rightabout or reversed, the image might be seen from a new perspective but the mirror is not reflecting anything new. In fact, the women reflected in it are to all intents and purposes, stuck at the same point as Lacan's child in "The Mirror Stage,"[1] who recognizes and assumes a specular image of himself at a stage of development "before the language restores to it [the I], in the universal, its function as subject" (p. 2). For these women do not achieve their function as subject of their own language but remain the eternal object of the language of men, reflected by this language and assuming this fictional identity projected in front of their eyes as their full reality, rather than a primary image against which to react and form their sense of self. Lacan continues:

> [But] the important point is that this form [the Ideal-I] situates the agency of the ego, before its social determination, in a fictional direction, which will always remain irreducible for the individual alone, or rather, which will only rejoin the coming-into-being (le devenir) of the subject asymptotically, whatever the success of the dialectical syntheses by which he must resolve as *I* his discordance with his own reality. (p. 2)

So all egos set off from a fictitious base, but given the nature of the social determination allowed to girls, they are very unlikely to gain any usefully realistic image of themselves within the patriarchal structure.

Realizing this, the authors we have considered here move gradually away from any attempt to find a new angle on the descriptions men have provided for them and begin to take the advice given by Alysse in *The Euguélionne*, when she is searching for her identity also.

> 71. But whatever effort you may make you will not be able to remember your *real* name, unless you get out of the Magic Circle
> . . .
> 75. And how do you get out of the Magic Circle? I asked Alysse

Come-Back-From. "You must break the glass," said Alysse. "The Magic Circle is a Mirror. You must break the magic of the Mirror."
"Can't you go through it?"
"That's how you get in," replied Alysse. "I tried it myself. But what I found was only the reverse of things. I found nothing NEW. So I broke the mirror to get out."

And this is what Bersianik has done — provided not a new mirror, but new eyes. With new eyes come new perceptions, new reactions. The rejected system is no longer accepted tacitly by the acceptance of the role of outcast (witch) but refused actively by transgression. Bersianik's women break the laws men have made to their disadvantage, thus they reject the male description of society and provide their own, based on the equal human-ness of women and men.

If they are equal, then all situations should be reversible, all roles interchangeable. However, as we have seen in the previous chapter, when most daily occurrences are described with the roles the other way around, they become ludicrous and the world becomes a parody of itself. Injustices of all sizes leap to the eye, behaviour patterns that are ridiculous, offensive, inacceptable. Like the Lady of Shalott, Bersianik's women are sick of shadows; they are no longer satisfied by the reflections of the world provided by the mirrors men have given them, and they have finally walked over to the window to look for themselves.

The result is a total reassessment of what life is about, a fresh and active writing/reading of a story that had finally been recognized as unsatisfactory because of over-insistent telling.

Or, to restate the process in the words of Mary Daly:[2]

> In the course of this Voyage, we have seen that patriarchy is designed not only to possess women, but to preposses/preoccupy us, that is, to inspire women with false selves which anesthetize the Self, breaking the process of be-ing on the wheel of processions. This condensing and freezing of be-ing into fragmented being is the necessary condition for maintaining the State of Possession. Condensation, or thing-ifying, makes "ownership" of Female Divinity possible, in the sense that it erases our awareness of this, our Process, and blocks our original movement. Yet it is not possible to own/possess Process itself. The confusion that is evoked in all women as a result of sensing simultaneously both the invincible reality of Female Process itself and its erasure/

fragmentation in the foreground of our consciousness is the condition of being spooked. (p. 322)

And here both the "spooking" and "negative spooking" are done by means of language. As Daly says:

> ... male controlled language in all matters pertaining to gynocentric identity: the words simply do not exist. In such a situation it is difficult even to imagine the right questions about our situation. Women struggling for words feel haunted by false feelings of personal inadequacy, by anger, frustration, and a kind of sadness/ bereavement. For it is, after all, our "mother tongue" that has been turned against us by the tongue-twisters. Learning to speak our Mothers' Tongue *is* exorcising the male "mothers." (p. 330)

Therefore, women authors are having to create a language for themselves to break out of the silence imposed by their "mother tongue." Symbolically, they have to become witches — crones Daly would say — and regain the power of words that has been taken from them. Fighting against all social and literary structures, as they always did in the past:

> The spookiness of this situation is intensified by the fact that women's minds are constantly being filled with debased images of Crones. These range from the "wicked step-mother" images injected through fairy tales and Hallowe'en caricatures of witches to the mother-in-law jokes that "enliven" parties and TV "situation comedies." (p. 350)

these witches have to overwhelm the "token women" of the patriarchy — princesses, dead queens and step-mothers — to take over their stories once more.

Likewise their readers are learning to look and judge for themselves; they are gradually throwing off the good, attentive schoolgirl attitude and ceasing to let themselves be impressed by traditional authoritative speech, for when they look closely they see that half of it is empty rhetoric and the rest self-interested manipulation. This is what the reclaiming of literature in *Les Guérillères* and *The Euguélionne* is all about. Instead of believing what they are told, women are thinking about what they hear and read, ready to criticize from their point of view and to change what they find inacceptable.

*****

With this idea of active re-writing for oneself in mind, and a memory of Bettleheim's interpretation of fairy tales in the background, I should like to offer in lieu of a formal conclusion a little story which serves as the perfect note on which to end this book. It is called *A bad reading* and is by Constance Delaunay.[3]

A little girl is re-reading "Bluebeard." First she sees herself in a mirror — playing at being the heroine:

> At this moment it is she, the little girl herself, who is parading in front of the mirror where she sees what she could not describe (she: a lady). (p. 10)

But then she catches sight of her shoes, little girl shoes instead of those "that *every* mother is buying for her daughter," and the apparent reflection on her powerlessness and the way she is being prevented from growing up sparks off a revolt, because the description of the shoes is followed by:

> It is then that Lady Bluebeard whose story, stupidity, blunder she knows, seems to her more idiotic than ever . . . All she had to do, when the misfortune she should have foreseen occurs, is wail and repent into the bargain, beg for mercy (action beneath contempt), then call that other imbecile, her sister Anne, to come to her aid. (p. 11)

She would not have done such a thing; she would have cut Bluebeard's head off as he came through the door.

This decided, she reads on: the other girls were afraid of him, they told tales about his wives and so on. Suddenly it is she who is in the room with the dead women. The last of them was blonde — all fairy tale heroines are blonde, blue-eyed, pale skinned and delicate, and they are all dead — very different from the little girl looking at them, and whose scorn for their passive acceptance of male dominance comes pouring out:

> Go on then, cry, silly fool . . . You are crying because you are afraid. You regret what you saw because now he wants to, he must, kill you. At no time does it occur to you to defend yourself. To sell your life dearly. To accuse him in your turn. That key, you didn't steal it from him. (p. 17)

This outburst is followed by a certain spirit of comradeship for Bluebeard: "Poor Bluebeard: his adversary is not of his stature. Not a word, not a single gesture of hatred or defiance" (p. 18). After all, man needs an equal against whom he can test himself. She would be that worthy opponent. Dressed in the dress of one of the murdered wives she watches for his arrival in her mirror in order to see his reaction and decide what to do. Either he will drop dead from shock, thinking one of his victims has returned, or she must act:

> She drops the casket which falls with a noise of broken glass. She has just time to twist and dive at the very moment he jumps at her. She grabs his feet. He stumbles and falls, his legs caught in his travelling cape.
> Drawing the sword from the scabbard, she stands upright, presses the point down between his shoulder blades and, straining, both hands firmly on the cross-piece of the pommel, pushes down with all her might. The sword sinks in, the little girl lets go. (pp. 20-21)

Here the mirror no longer reflects the princess' passiveness — we are told explicitly that the girl's features are not visible in it — but (as in Wittig) the prince, facing his behaviour vis-a-vis his wives: man the murderer is revealed in his turn. She no longer admires herself, motionless in the glass, preening as in the beginning of the story, but uses it actively to gain information from which she can act.

The minute she moves the glass breaks, for it has no further use. The old image of the passive heroine has gone forever. The girl is free. Indeed, she expresses her new found freedom very clearly:

> Tearing off the little gold key attached by a cord to her belt, she forces it between his teeth, where a few pink bubbles are foaming. (p. 21)

The key of her captivity has been literally stuffed down the jailor's throat.
And the little girl reads on to the moral of the story. "Il y en a deux" we are told,

> There are two ... as if the author, having scolded the little girls gently, changed his mind and decided to speak seriously about their future even if he left the dreamers perplexed. (p. 21)

A double standard. One for the "cruches," the dead princesses, the little girls who behave like dolls, and one for the likes of our reader:

> There is no husband so terrible
> Nor who requires the impossible
> Be he discontented and jealous . . . (p. 21)

For the latter, there are no despotic husbands. She is the summation of the heroines we have seen, and if everybody read as she does, retaining control over the language of the book and thereby retaining power over its content, there would be no "pédaleuses," no princesses and no divided selves.

* * * * *

Women are throwing off their education, disregarding authority and rather regarding all existent language (public speech especially) as being full of traps laid to keep them in the subordinate roles men have found convenient. All literature must now be regarded with suspicion, analysed for the author's *real* intention, albeit indirectly or unconsciously expressed, so that the extent of the subliminal pressure women are under constantly, is stated clearly. Only then can the culturally based confusion in the midst of which they live be eliminated. Women can then be secure in an identity free of the overtones and innuendo that constantly reverse the apparent description of themselves given at the moment, creating the incompatible demands between which they are caught.

The world is the way it is because it has been told that way, and it is being reaffirmed in that form all the time by frequent retelling. Women hold inferior status in it because they are constantly described in subordinate positions and everybody is affected by the descriptions that surround her/him, for we have all been taught to trust in the word.

Clearly, if the present state of affairs exists through language, then the power base of change is language also. And this is seen to be of prime importance in the novels we have looked at. To silence them, women were masked and threatened with the label "mad" and this label, bringing with it as it did the horror of social exile, worked for a while. But as Foucault observed in another context in *Madness and Civilization*,[4] madness develops a dynamic of its own and after a while,

> . . . all that is present is the most internal, and at the same time the

most savagely free, of forces . . . Beyond that point, the faces themselves decompose; this is no longer the madness of the *Caprichos*, which tied on masks truer than the truth of faces; this is a madness *beneath* the mask, a madness that eats away faces, corrodes features; there are no longer eyes or mouths, but glances shot from nowhere and staring at nothing (as in the *Witches' Sabbath*); or screams from black holes (as in the *Pilgrimage of Saint Isidore*). *Madness has become man's possibility of abolishing both man and the world — and even those images that challenge the world and deform man.* It is, far beyond dreams, beyond the nightmare of bestiality, the last recourse: the end and the beginning of everything. (p. 281. My emphasis)

Man's possibility first, and now woman's possibility, for now as then, through the madness depicted,

> . . . a work that seems to drown in the world, to reveal there its non-sense, and to transfigure itself with the features of pathology alone, actually engages within itself the world's time, masters it, and leads it; by the madness which interrupts it, a work of art opens a void, a moment of silence, a question without answer, provokes a breach without reconciliation where the world is forced to question itself. What is necessarily a profanation in the work of art returns to that point, and, in the time of that work swamped in madness, the world is made aware of its guilt. Henceforth, and through the mediation of madness, it is the world that becomes culpable (for the first time in the Western world) in relation to the work of art; it is now arraigned by the work of art, obliged to order itself by its language, compelled by it to a task of recognition, of reparation, to the task of restoring reason *from* that unreason and *to* that unreason. (p. 288)

Foucault was writing about insane male writers, but what he says is applicable here on two counts: the first, that a number of the characters we have studied have come to terms with such madness and changed the world thereby; the second, that as all women are alienated to some extent by the patriarchal structures of society, all works written by women are perforce by mad women.

In this book we have watched this definition of woman's problem emerge gradually over two countries and nearly a quarter of a century of writing. Little by little we have seen marriage cease to be seen as an end in itself and its abusive practices questioned. Woman's frustration within her traditional role has also changed its expression. At first, martyrdom or self-destruction through well or badly disguised schizophrenia, her refusal of this amalgamation of slavery and decorative unobtrusiveness has gradually become more active, even violent, and also vocal. The women grow in self-assurance, setting their own priorities, selecting their own images. The fairy tale race is evolving and the witch is being rehabilitated, but, as we have seen, for the most part the influence of the fairy tale, together with its cultural reinforcements, is still very much the centre of woman's imagination and self-perception. Her self-definition and description are still created with reference to patriarchal patterns. In a sense, each author and heroine studied here is still asking:

"Mirror, mirror on the wall,
How do I compare with the fairest of us all?" (i.e., men)

Even the Euguélionne and her disciples are in this position, because they have Freud, Jahweh and Christ against whom to measure themselves.

We are still in a world of binary oppositions, in a competitive situation in which there is bound to be a first sex, followed, therefore, by the inevitable second. Language and thought in the Western world have developed in that form; good/bad, male/female, strong/weak, active/passive and so *ad infinitum* — and the fairy tales are some of the most widely known illustrations of this system.

Clearly, something has to be done to prevent future generations of children from being given this as the first (and most effective) structure on which to model not only their day-dreams but also, and more importantly, the very functioning of their imagination. The problem is a very difficult one to resolve however, as it involves the creation of an equivalent body of children's literature which incorporates all the strengths of faëry and none of its unacceptable social conditioning. Perhaps Constance Delaunay has set a valid example when her heroine takes for herself a life of action similar to that of Bluebeard, the hero.

Solutions are not yet evident, but perhaps the examination of the novels in this book has clarified the issue, and revealed where the struggle for equality, sanity and right to action must take place. The field is open to a generation liberated from the stereotypic, deprecatory images of themselves as dead princess, social outcast or madwoman. The myth of female weakness has been rejected at source; the myth of power remains and so does the way of action for those who do not need to seek reassurances in any glass.

It is fitting that this essay should end with a radical re-description of the situation it has tried to clarify. I give the last word to Mary Daly:

In their house of mirrors, the past-owners/past-makers constantly bombard women's minds with false and insignificant choices in order to prevent us from seeing/facing the real choices that further our escaping, Self-enspiriting, and bonding with other women. The spookers attempt to possess and destroy the future by haunting women's minds *now*, preventing our Presence in our present. We have seen that they administer such preventive medicine by destroying and remaking the past, inspiring women with lies, with fears, with the disease of caution and self-contempt. There is no sharp line between the possessed "past" and the possessed "future," since both are illusions which constantly separate and re-blend, reflecting each other repeatedly, echoing each other endlessly. Keeping this blur in mind, Hags can crack the "future" mirror.

The basic form of the father's funereal "future" is fear. The necrophiliac Prince Charmings keep their Snow White spouses in the State of Sleeping Death with promises of a fear-free future. This blend of male-made fear and promise of release from fear is the recipe for the poison in the Poisoned Apples foisted upon females by the "Wicked Queens." Every Hag who has escaped from the glass coffin and dependent dwarfs intended for us has come to know the true identity of the poison-pushing Queen: "She," that is, he, is the archetypal Drag Queen, the male stepmother, the other side of Prince Charming's multiple personality, his holy ghost. He is able to trick the princess because he dissembles, falsely re-sembling the true Queen, the Wild Witch, the dis-membered Goddess.

Since the feigned future which is used to make women faint-hearted, faint-minded, fixed in a permanent faint is a shadow world, a world of deceptive lights and shadows, it is useless to strike at it directly. Instead of shadow-boxing, the gynaesthetic traveler learns to detect the deceptive light-projector, the shadow-caster. She detects the pattern that is behind his deceptive patterns; she dis-covers the necrophiliac nature of the fear in which he is fixated, which is also the fear he projects upon/injects into his snow white victims. This is *not* the fear of dying but the fear of living. As Valerie Solanas lucidly points out: "The male likes death — it excites him sexually and, already dead inside, he wants to die." This statement would seem to be adequately substantiated/documented by the state of this male-controlled planet. If patriarchal males loved life, the planet would be different.

Most precisely, the wicked drag queens' fear is fear of Female Living, of female-identified biophilic energy. For the release of this energy will mean the end of their blissful State of Sleeping Death. They therefore are compelled to use every means at hand to perpetuate the State of Paralysis. We have already discussed some of their tranquilizing treatments, their haunting holding patterns. One pattern common to all of these patterns is imposed poverty. The male queens perpetually try to keep women "blessed" by poverty of spirit. We have seen that they have starved women's minds through transmitting a poor vocabulary, a shabby symbol system, a genuinely impoverishing education. Hags can hardly afford to overlook the fact that they keep us chained to the wheel of mind-deadening work by keeping us economically poor. Our spiritual and physical deprivation/poverty nourish and support each other. The queens/prince charmings thus work to keep women road-blocked by the twin rocks of spiritual and economic poverty.

Depressed and angry over this unjust impoverishment, women at first turn our anger against ourselves and each other, blaming each other for being "richer" or "poorer" in different ways. Locked in mortal combat with ourselves and each other, we are kept from living in the Female Present/Presence. As long as this spooking trick works, the queens succeed in maintaining the State of Sleeping Death, where women are encased in the glass coffins of false past and false future.

Spinsters smash our way out of the mirror coffins by our courageous/contagious Revolting Risking. Our reckless Risking is unlike the ruthless "bravery" of the necrophiliac bombmakers, planet-polluters, who try to turn the earth into their Poisoned Apple. The Life-loving Risking of Hags means loving our Selves and therefore turning our anger into propelling power for the Journey. Recognizing, finally, that we have all been possessed in the State of Possession, Furies can begin to stop misfiring our Fury at each other. Recognizing that we have been made falsely rich and truly poor in a vast variety of ways, we can learn to overcome the spooking confusion and Self-defeating conflicts over our diverse situations which are not of our own making. Not insipid "tolerance" but strong truthfulness about such complex conditions will enable Furious women to bond and to move deeper into the Background. (pp. 351-53)

NOTES

CHAPTER 1

[1] This chapter was published in the *International Journal of Women's Studies*, vol. 2, no. 2, March/April 1979.

[2] Simone de Beauvoir, *Le Deuxième Sexe*, Paris, Gallimard, 1949. *The Second Sex*, New York, Alfred A. Knopf, 1964, trans. H.M. Parshley.

[3] Simone de Beauvoir, *Mémoires d'un jeune fille rangée*, Paris, Gallimard, 1958. *Memoirs of a dutiful daughter:* quoted with comment in Michèle Le Doeuff, "Women and Philosophy," *Radical Philosophy*, 17, Summer 1977, p. 8.

[4] Bruno Bettelheim, *The Uses of Enchantment*, New York, Vintage Books, 1977. All references will be to this edition.

[5] Mary Daly, *Gyn/Ecology: The Metaethics of Radical Feminism*, Boston, Beacon Press, 1978. All references will be to this edition.

[6] R.D. Laing, *The Divided Self*, Harmondsworth, Penguin Books, 1971. All references will be to this edition.

[7] Phyllis Chesler, *Women and Madness*, New York, Avon Books, 1973. As one example I quote Chesler quoting Thomas Szasz, p. 101:

> Witches and mentally ill patients are actually created through the social interaction of oppressors and oppressed. If the observer sympathizes with the oppressor, then the witches are "mad." If the observer sympathizes with the victim, then the oppressor is "mad." Both explanations bypass, conceal, excuse and explain away the terrifyingly simple but all important fact of man's inhumanity to man [and I add: to woman] . . . the image of the knight in armour, the symbol of mobility, and of the black witch as a symbol of depravity embodies the sexocidal hatred of women . . . [for the] knight is always male [and the] witch is always female

in all the fairy tales and mythologies of (medieval and modern) times.

[8] Mary Daly, pp. 90-91:

Children's books provide chilling evidence of mind-control through dismembering myth. Fairy tales are particularly gruesome examples. An apparently genteel contemporary type of disguised mind-dismembering myth for children is exemplified in *The Giving Tree*, by Shel Silverstein. It is the story of a tree — consistently referred to by the pronoun she — who gives absolutely everything she has to a boy. This begins innocently enough, with her shade, leaves, and fruit. But, the boy grows up and cuts off her branches and then her trunk. Finally, in his old age, he uses her stump as a seat. As a result of all this nonreciprocated giving, the tree is "happy."

The jacket blurb of this book, published in 1964 but still a big seller, describes it as "a tender story . . . a moving parable for readers of all ages." The story, in fact, is one of female rape and dismemberment. It draws upon sources in the Background of female identity, taking the Tree of Life — who is the Goddess — and making her a willing participant in her own mutilation, which makes her "happy." Her degradation is total, for the "Giving Tree" wallows in self-destruction. Here is a model of masochism for female readers of all ages, and of sadism for boys of all ages. This chilling children's tale is an extension of christian myth. It is a superrefined, invasive, and deceptive offspring of self-satisfied secularists secure in their superiority to Christian crudity. The saccharine sweet story of a little boy who "loves" a tree — a young Apollo who crowns himself with her leaves — has "healthier" appeal than overt S and M biblical tales of a dead godman crowned with thorns. Thus the post-christian (that is prechristian) parable has deceptive acceptability, extending its tentacles into unaware minds, guiding them to a more primal Fatherland, inhabited by paradigms of patriarchal matricide. It thus brings its parental purchasers and readers into unwitting compliance with primary programming for gynocide.

Whether or not the authors, illustrators, and promotors of such books "understand" that they are communicating gynocidal messages is beside the point. Since self-deception is of the essence of doublethink, they undoubtedly would respond with incredulity/

amusement/indignation to such an analysis. For they themselves have been programmed not to recognize gynodical reversals. Within the massive public relations business of patriarchy, the promotion of rape and dismemberment has top priority, and it is essential that the promoters make this fact invisible to everyone, especially to themselves. As George Orwell wrote of his character, Winston Smith, in *1984*: "For the first time he perceived that if you want to keep a secret you must also hide it from yourself."

[9] Andrea Dworkin, *Woman Hating*, New York, Dutton Books, 1976, and Daly, pp. 134-52.
[10] Chesler, p. 30:

> Persephone does not wish to be raped, nor do women today. Neither do they wish to recapitulate their mother's identity. But the modern Persephone still has no other place to go but into marriage and motherhood. Her father (men in general) still conforms to a rape-incest model of sexuality. And her mother has not taught her to be a warrior, i.e., to take difficult roads to unknown and unique destinations — gladly. Her mother and father neither prepare her for this task nor rejoice in her success.

[11] Marie-Louise von Franz, *The Feminine in Fairy Tales*, Zurich and New York, Spring Pubs., 1972, and numerous other titles.
[12] James Hillman, "First Adam, Then Eve," *Eranos Jahr Buch*, vol. 38, 1969, pp. 349-412.
[13] Chesler, p. 105:

> Szasz notes the similarity of zeal with which inquisitors and psychiatrists hunt and classify (or diagnose) witches and mental patients . . . Armed with a fearful knowledge of illness and sinfulness, both the Holy Father (the inquisitor) and the Scientific Father (the psychiatrist) are interested in saving female souls. Their methods: confession, recantation, and punishment. Of course, modern psychiatrists would not think that "helping" an "unhappy" woman accept her feminine role is at all similar to "helping" a witch return to Christ.

[14] Laing, p. 190, and *Sanity, Madness and the Family*, Harmondsworth, Penguin Books, 1970.

[15] Hillman, pp. 359-60:

> The female provides the *prima materia*, the nourishment and the place for the developing embryo. She has her necessary role. But the active, formative, generative principle comes wholly from the father. His is the better part. It would seem to be an equality in the sense of a parallelism or symmetry of function, but if we look a bit deeper we see the prejudice at work.
>
> The female contribution is menstrual blood, which after all is widely held to be taboo stuff, a wastage or at best a cleanser. Its inferiority to male semen is explicitly explained in Aristotle's theory of semen . . . The female contribution is therefore psychologically inferior. Besides having no seed she is without the *cause formalis* that can generate her own essence out of herself. Her essence is thus subject to the male, in whose essence is male and female both. As in the Genesis myth, in the male is the preformation of the female. First Adam, then Eve.

[16] Quoted in Le Doeuff, p. 5.
[17] Editions Fernand Nathan, Quoted in Suzy Verger, *Pipi debout, quelle injustice!*, Paris, Grasset, 1977, p. 93.

CHAPTER 2

[1] Anne Hébert, *Les Chambres de bois*, Paris, Editions du Seuil, 1958; *The Silent Rooms*, Don Mills, Musson Book Co., 1974, trans. Kathy Mezei. All references will be to the translated edition.

CHAPTER 3

[1] Part of this chapter has appeared under the title "Plus ça change . . ." in *Perspectives*, vol. 55 (Speed, Time and Change), University of Louisville, 1980. Simone de Beauvoir, *Les Belles Images*, Paris, Gallimard, 1966, and *Les Belles Images*, London, Wm. Collins Sons & Co., 1968, trans. Patrick O'Brian. All references will be to the translated edition.
[2] Simone de Beauvoir, *Le Deuxième Sexe*, tome 2, Paris, Gallimard, 1949, and *The Second Sex*, New York, Alfred A. Knopf, 1964, trans. H.M.

Parshley. All references are to this translation and identified by S.S. wherever necessary to avoid ambiguity.
³ "Une belle mécanique," *La Quinzaine Littéraire* no. 18, 15 Dec. 1966, p. 5.
⁴ For example,"Les Belles Images de Simone de Beauvoir," *Le Magazine Littéraire*, January 1967, pp. 45-46.
⁵ Jacqueline Piatier, "Simone de Beauvoir présente *Les Belles Images*," *Le Monde* no. 6826, 23 Dec. 1966, p. 17.
⁶ *Le Figaro Littéraire* 22 an., no. 1124, 30 Oct. -5 Nov. 1967, p. 29.
⁷ See *The Second Sex*, pp. 529-530 & 593.

CHAPTER 4

¹ This chapter, in a slightly different form, has been published under the title "Beauty and madness in M—C Blais' *La Belle Bête*" in *Journal of Canadian Fiction*, nos. 25/26, special issue *Les Romanciers Québecois et leurs oeuvres*, Winter, 1979, pp. 186-198.
² Marie-Claire Blais, *La Belle Bête*, Quebec C.L.F. poche, 1959. *Mad Shadows*,Toronto, McClelland & Stewart Limited, 1971, trans. Merloyd Lawrence. All further references will be to this translation.
³ R. D. Laing, *The Divided Self*, Harmondsworth, Penguin Books, 1965 edition, henceforth referred to in the text as Laing.
⁴ Phyllis Chesler, *Women and Madness*, New York, Avon Books, 1972, p. 265.

CHAPTER 5

¹ *Le Ravissement de Lol V. Stein*, Paris, Gallimard, 1964 and Folio 1976. *The Rapture of Lol V. Stein*, London, Hamish Hamilton, 1967, trans. Eileen Ellenbogen. (This translation is quite free, occasionally inaccurate and should be checked against the original text on all major points.) Reference in the text is to the translation except where indicated.
² Marc Soriano, *Les Contes de Perrault*, Paris, Gallimard, TEL, 1977, pp. 129-130.
³ No contact, no body, no suffering, no expression, no words; somebody else's language. Is this the reason for the curiously evocative and formal games that seem to be offered by the names in the novel? The clue is given by the names of the towns where Lol lives: S. Tahla, T. Beach, U. Bridge. This game is

played within a fixed and pre-established order — that of the alphabet. Let us set out the list.

A — Anne Marie; B — Beugner; but these seem to be marginal. The real list starts:

    H Hold
    I (self)
    J Jean, Jacques
    K Karl
    L Lola
    M Michael, Anne-Marie
    N
    O
    P Pierre
    Q *(cul)*
    R Richardson, *Ravissement*
    S S. Tahla, Stein, Stretter, Rapture
    T T. Beach, Tatiana
    U U. Bridge, (you), *(ou/où)*
    V Valerie

All kinds of messages can be obtained from this in English and a certain number in French. If we read them off we get: "Hold I Jacques", an ungrammatical appeal but an appeal nonetheless. Then the grouping Jean, Karl, Lola, Michael followed by the correction NO Pierre, putting the married couples together, or Jacques, Karl, Lola, Michael, NO, thus breaking up the lovers. Richardson is followed by Stein or Stretter. S. Tahla, T. Beach and U. Bridge follow in chronological order (U. *Bridge* recalling Bed*ford*) leading to Lol V. Stein.

Alternatively if we read in French, Q becomes "cul" and we read Jean, Karl, Lola, Michael, NO (Pierre), Q, followed by the reason: Richardson, Stein/Stretter, T. Beach, U. Bridge. U becomes ou/où and we see Stein, Tatiana ou Valerie: their unity is being either established or questioned. (The English gives a less equivocal message; pidgin style: Tatiana you Valerie.) Elsewhere we are given   Lola ⟵⟶ Stein
          Tatiana ⤫ Karl
and S. Tahla could be interpreted as "est Ta (Tatiana) là?" or as "Est-ce t'es là?" and "Reste-là" also. Both of which comment with pertinancy on Lol's condition and situation. So indeed does her name. She calls herself Lol—loll during her passive stage, emerging as Lola — *l'eau- là* as she achieves feeling and sexual expression, yet the full form which is, significantly, not in the novel is Lola V.—*l'eau, la vie;* the growth is as yet incomplete. Sleeping Beauty is shut

into a tower, for Lol the *tower* of her own *body*; shut into the tower of language: the *Tower* of *B*abel, and we have come full circle to *T. B*each.

CHAPTER 6

[1] C. Clément/H. Cixous, *La Jeune Née*, Paris, Union Générale D'Editions (10/18) 1975. My translation.

[2] See also Ida Magli's "Pouvoir de la parole et silence de la femme," *Cahiers du GRIF* (Brussels), no. 12, June 1976, pp. 37-43.

[3] Lewis Carroll, *Through the Looking Glass*, Chapter 6.

[4] Monique Wittig, *Le Corps Lesbien*, Paris, Les Editions de Minuit, 1973, and *The Lesbian Body*, New York, William Morrow, 1975, trans. David Le Vay.

[5] Mary Daly, *Gyn/Ecology*, p. 231.

[6] About her, Mary Daly writes:

In essence, the Spinster is a witch. She is derided because she is free and therefore feared. Since derision is not powerful enough to stop her spinning, she is the object of attack by propaganda. Any cursory reading of a typical children's fairy tale book gives overwhelming evidence of the campaign against witches, which includes mothers, stepmothers, wicked queens, ogresses. It is not accidental that in the story of Sleeping Beauty, the princess is cursed to prick her finger on a spindle which causes her to fall asleep for one hundred years, until she is awakened by her prince. More adept Spinsters are not falling asleep, not waiting to be awakened, but awakening and waking each other by our Presence. (p. 394)

For further comments see also pp. 178-222, "European Witch-burnings: Purifying the Body of Christ."

[7] Luce Irigaray, *Ce sexe qui n'en est pas un,** Paris, Les Editions de Minuit, Collection Critique, 1977. All future references will be to this edition and translations are my own.

[8] Michel Foucault, *La volonté de savoir*, Paris, Editions Gallimard, Collection Bibliothèque des Histoires, 1977. My translation. Now published as *The History of Sexuality*, New York, Pantheon Books, 1978, trans. Robert Hurley.

* Extracts of these texts are now available in *New French Feminisms* ed. Elaine Marks and Isabelle de Courtivron, University of Massachusetts Press, Amherst, 1980.

[9] Elizabeth Janeway, *Man's World Woman's Place*, Harmondsworth, Penguin Books, 1977.

CHAPTER 7

[1] J. Hyvrard, *Les Prunes de Cythère*, Paris, Les Editions de Minuit, 1975. All translations are mine and the page references are to the French edition. Part of this chapter was given as a paper to the APFUC at Saskatoon, May 1979 and published in a slightly different form in a paper entitled "He asked for her hand in marriage" in *New York Literary Forum* special issue on *Fragmentation* (1981).

[2] See for example "Les Québecoises," *Room of One's Own* (Vancouver) vol 4, nos 1 & 2, Winter 1978, which is a special issue containing translations from "Le corps, les mots, l'imaginaire," *La Barre du Jour*, nos. 56-57, May-August 1977.

[3] "Corps—Mort," *La Barre du Jour*, nos. 56-57, pp. 68-82 and in *Room of One's Own*, vol 4 nos. 1 & 2, pp. 44-54, trans. Josée M. LeBlond.

[4] Monique Wittig, *Les Guérillères*, Paris, Les Editions de Minuit, 1969. *Les Guérillères*, New York, The Viking Press, 1977, trans. David Le Vay. All quotations are from this translation. Part of this chapter is to be published under the title "Circle Games in M. Wittig's *Les Guérillères*," *Perspectives*, University of Louisville, 1982.

[5] Mary Daly, *Gyn/Ecology*, pp. 10-11:

> I am using the term *Gyn/Ecology* very loosely, that is, freely, to describe the science, that is the process of know-ing, of "loose" women who choose to be subjects and not mere objects of enquiry. Gyn/Ecology is by and about women a-mazing all the male-authored "sciences of womankind," and weaving world tapestries *of our own kind.* That is, it is about dis-covering, de-veloping the complex web of living/loving relationships *of our own kind*. It is about women living, loving, creating our Selves, our cosmos. It *is* dis-possessing our Selves, enspiriting our Selves, hearing the call of the wild, naming our wisdom, spinning and weaving world tapestries out of genesis and demise. In contrast to gynecology, which depends upon fixation and dismemberment, Gyn/Ecology affirms that everything is connected.

Since "o-logies" are generally static "bodies of knowledge," it might at first glance seem that the name *Gyn/Ecology* clashes with the theme of the Journey. However, a close analysis unveils the fact that this is not so. For women can recognize the powerful and multidimensional gynocentric symbolism of the "O." It represents the power of our moving, encircling presence, which can make nonbeing sink back into itself. Our "O" is totally other than "nothing" (a fact demonically distorted and reversed in the pornographic novel, *The Story of O*). As Denise Connors has pointed out, it can be taken to represent our aura, our O-Zone. Within this antipollutant, purifying, moving O-Zone, the aura of gynocentric consciousness, life-loving feminists have the power to affirm the basic Gyn/Ecological principle that everything is connected with everything else. It is this holistic process of knowing that can make Gyn/Ecology the O-logy of all the -ologies, encircling them, spinning around and through them, unmasking their emptiness. As the O-logy of all the -ologies, Gyn/Ecology can reduce their pretentious facades to Zero. It can free the flow of their "courses" and overcome their necrophilic circles, their self-enclosed processions, through spiraling creative process. It is women's own Gyn/Ecology that can break their brokenness of the "fields," deriding their borders and boundaries, changing the nouns of knowledge into verbs of know-ing.

CHAPTER 8

[1] Louky Bersianik, *L'Euguélionne*, Montreal, Les Editions la Presse, 1976. All translations are my own. The Euguélionne is now available in English however: trans G. Denis, A. Hewitt, D. Murray and M. O'brien, Victoria, Press Porcépic, 1981.

CHAPTER 9

[1] Jacques Lacan, *Ecrits*, "Le stade du miroir comme formateur de la fonction du Je," Paris, Editions du Seuil, 1966; and *Ecrits, A selection*, "The mirror stage as formative of the function of the I as revealed in psychoanalytic experience," London, Tavistock Publications, 1977, trans. Alan Sheridan. Quotations are from this translation.

² Mary Daly, *Gyn/Ecology*. All references to Daly in this chapter are from this book.

³ Constance Delaunay, "Une Mauvaise Lecture," in *Une Mauvaise Lecture*, Paris, Editions Gallimard, 1967. All translations are mine.

⁴ Michel Foucault, *Histoire de la folie*, Paris, Librairie Plon, 1961; and *Madness and Civilization*, New York, Vintage Books, 1973, trans. Richard Howard. The quotations are taken from the latter.

AN IDIOSYNCRATIC BIBLIOGRAPHY

(Most of the books and papers listed here have been chosen for the references they contain in their turn.)

Beauvoir, Simone de; *Le deuxième sexe*, Paris, Gallimard, 1949. *Mémoires d'une jeune fille rangée*, Paris, Gallimard, 1958.

Belotti, Gianini; *Du côté des petites filles*, Paris, Des Femmes, 1974.

Bettelheim, Bruno; *The Uses of Enchantment*, New York, Vintage Books, 1977.

Boucher, Denise/Gagnon, Madeleine; *Retailles* complaintes politiques, Montreal, Les Editions l'Etincelle, 1977.

Brée, Germaine; *French Women Writers:* a problematic perspective, New York, Mackay, Collection Joan I. Roberts, 1976.

Bullough, Vern L.; *The subordinate Sex:* a history of attitudes towards women, Baltimore, Penguin Books, 1974.

Burke, Carolyn Greenstein; "Report from Paris: Women's writing and the Women's Movement," *Signs* Vol. 3, No. 4, Summer 1978, pp. 843-55.

Chesler, Phyllis; *Women and Madness*, New York, Avon Books, 1973.

Cixous, Hélène; "Le rire de la Méduse," *Simone de Beauvoir et la lutte des femmes, L'Arc*, No. 61, 1975. Reprinted as "The Laugh of the Medusa" trans. Gohen, Keith and Paula, *Signs*, Vol. 1, No. 4, Summer 1976, pp. 875-93.

Clément, Catherine; "Enclave esclave," *Simone de Beauvoir et la lutte des femmes, L'Arc*, No. 61. 1975.

"La coupable," *La Jeune Née*, Paris, Union Générale d'Editions, 1975. and Irigaray, Luce; "La femme, son sexe et sa langue," *La Nouvelle Critique*, No. 82, March 1975, pp. 36-9.

Daly, Mary; *Beyond God the Father*, Boston, Beacon Press, 1973. *Gyn/Ecology; The Metaethics of Radical Feminism*, Boston, Beacon Press, 1978.

Duffy, Maureen; *The Erotic World of Faery*, London, Hodder and Stoughton, 1972.

Dworkin, Andrea; *Woman Hating*, New York, E.P. Dutton Inc., 1974.

Felman, Shoshana; "Women and Madness: the critical phallacy," *Diacritics* Vol. 5, No. 3, Winter 1975, pp. 2-10.

Foucault, Michel; *The History of Sexuality*, New York, Pantheon Books, 1978. *Madness & Civilization*, New York, Random House, 1965.

Fox, Geer Litton; " 'Nice Girl': Social Control of Women through a Value Construct," *Signs*, Vol. 2, No. 4, Summer 1977, pp. 805-17.

Franz, Marie-Louise von; *The Feminine in Fairytales*, Zurich and New York, Spring Publications, 1972.
Gagnon, Madeleine, Cixous, Hélène and Leclerc, Annie; *La venue à l'écriture*, Paris, Union Générale d'Editions, 1977.
Garrett, Clarke; "Women and Witches: Patterns of analysis," *Signs*, Vol. 3, No. 2, Winter 1977, pp. 461-70.
Gubar, Susan; "The Female Monster in Augustan Satire," *Signs*, Vol. 3, No. 2, Winter 1977, pp. 380-94.
Gutman, Colette; "Blanche-Neige en Trente Secondes," *Les Temps Modernes*, 31e année, No. 358, May 1976, pp. 1862-70.
Herrmann, Claudine; *Les Voleuses de Langue*, Paris, Des Femmes, 1976.
Hillman, James; "First Adam then Eve," *Eranos Jahr Buch*, Vol. 38, 1969, pp. 349-412.
Irigaray, Luce; *Ce sexe qui n'en est pas un*, Paris, Les Editions de Minuit, 1977.
Speculum de l'autre femme, Paris, Editions de Minuit, 1974.
Janeway, Elizabeth; *Man's World, Woman's Place*, Harmondsworth, Penguin Books, 1977.
Kramer, Chris, Thorne, Barrie and Henley, Nancy; "Perspectives on Language and Communications," *Signs*, Vol. 3, No. 3, Spring 1978, pp. 638-51.
Laing, R.D.; *The Divided Self*, Harmondsworth, Penguin Books, 1965.
The Politics of the Family, Harmondsworth, Penguin Books, 1976.
and Esterson, A.; *Sanity Madness and the Family*, Harmondsworth, Penguin Books, 1970.
Lakoff, Robin; *Language and Woman's Place*, New York, Harper and Row, 1975.
Le Doeuff, Michèle; "Women and Philosophy," *Radical Philosophy*, No. 17, Summer 1977.
Luthi, Max; *Once upon a time. On the nature of fairy tales*, trans. L. Chadeayne and P. Gottwald, Bloomington and London, Indiana University Press, 1970.
Magli, Ida; "Pouvoir de la parole et silence de la femme," *Cahiers du GRIF*, No. 12, June 1976, pp. 37-43.
Marini, Marcelle; *Territoires du féminin: écrire avec M. Duras*, Paris, Editions de Minuit, 1977.
Marks, Elaine; "Women and Literature in France," *Signs* Vol. 3, No. 4, Summer 1978, pp. 832-42.
and de Courtivron I. Ed., *New French Feminisms*, Amherst, Univ. of Massachusetts Press, 1980.
Miller, Jean Baker; *Toward a New Psychology of Women*, Harmondsworth, Penguin Books, 1976.

Montrelay, Michèle; L'*ombre et le nom*, Paris, Editions de Minuit, 1977.

Soriano, Marc; *Les contes de Perrault*, Paris, Gallimard, 1968.

Rossum-Guyon, Françoise van, and Mercier, Roger; *Ecriture, féminité, feminisme, Revue des Sciences humaines*, No. 168, Winter 1977.

Rowbotham, Sheila; *Woman's Consciousness, Man's World*, Harmondsworth, Penguin Books, 1973.

Ruether, Rosemary Radford; *New Woman New Earth:* sexist ideologies and human liberation, New York, Seabury Press, 1975.

Vergez, Suzy; *Pipi Debout, Quelle Injustice!* Paris, Grasset, 1977.

INDEX

Adam, 8, 78, 80, 101, 106, 117
Alice in Wonderland, 101, 116
Amazons, 135
Andersen, Hans, 5
Anne (*Mad Shadows*), 53-54, 56
Apocalypse, The, 18
Apollo, 147
apollonic structure, 8-9
Aristotle, 8, 11
Bathsheba, 103
"Beauty and the Beast," 2, 7, 10, 13-20, 23, 29, 58
Beauvoir, Simone de, 1, 10, 31-33, 34, 84, 115, 134, 146, 149-150
Belles Images, Les, 10, 31-44, 47, 56, 57, 134, 149-150
Bersianik, Louky, 76, 91, 113, 116, 132, 136, 154
Bettelheim, Bruno, 2-3, 4, 6, 8, 146
birth, 94, 126-127
Blais, Marie-Claire, 10, 45, 56, 85, 134, 150
blood, 86-88, 90, 94, 97-98, 122, 149
Bluebeard, 138, 140,142
Bosco, Monique, 91, 101, 104
Boucher, Denise, 101
Brigitte, 43-44, 47
Brossard, Nicole, 101
Carroll, Lewis, 76, 152
Catherine (*Les Belles Images*), 42-44, 47
Catherine (*The Silent Rooms*), 10, 13-30, 79, 84, 85, 89
Ce sexe qui n'en est pas un, 81-82, 83-84, 85-86, 88, 152
Chapsal, Madeleine, 31
Chesler, Phyllis, 146, 148, 150
Cinderella, 7, 10, 11, 45, 51, 55, 99, 102, 118
Circe, 81
Cixous, Hélène, 78, 152
Claudel, Paul, 120
Clément, Catherine, 152
Cloutier, Cécile, 101
Comte, Auguste, 11
Corps lesbien, Le, 80, 152

Culpepper, Emily, 80
Daly, Mary, 4, 79, 90, 136-137, 143, 146, 147, 152, 153
David and Goliath, 103
death, 3, 13, 14, 17, 18, 20, 22, 24-25, 28, 33, 44, 45, 61, 73, 78, 81, 96-97, 99, 101, 102, 103, 118, 124, 126, 133, 143
Delaunay, Constance, 91, 134, 142, 154
Demeter, 55-56
Dietrich, Marlene, 99
Divided Self, The, 6, 7, 8, 71-72, 146, 150
Duras, Marguerite, 10, 58, 74, 85, 134
Dworkin, Andrea, 148
Elle, 32
Encyclopédie de la femme, L', 12
Euguélionne, The, 76, 113-133, 134, 135-136, 137, 142, 154
Eve, 8, 78, 80, 101, 106, 114, 117, 130
fairytales, 1, 2, 4, 5, 6, 7, 8, 11, 13, 16, 17, 19, 23, 25-26, 30, 33, 35, 43, 45, 47, 55, 57, 73, 74, 80, 81, 82, 86, 88, 100, 101, 108-109, 118, 142, 147-148
father, 2-3, 5, 7, 13, 14, 15, 22, 24, 27, 42, 45, 52, 58, 63, 64, 65, 67, 78, 80, 83, 99, 115, 143
Faust, 46, 48
Femme rompue, La, 32
Foucault, Michel, 86, 88, 90, 140-141, 152, 155
Freud, 8, 22, 26, 129, 142
Friedan, Betty, 115
Gagnon, Madeleine, 101
Garbo, Greta, 99
Genesis, 8
Guérillières, Les, 92, 104-112, 113, 118, 137
Grail, The, 108
Grimm, The brothers, 5
Gyn/Ecology, 4, 79, 90, 136-137, 146, 147-148, 152, 153-154
hag, 9, 79, 143, 144

159

"Hans my Hedgehog", 2
Hébert, Anne, 10, 13, 134, 149
Hillman, James, 8-9, 148, 149
Hostage, The, 120
Humpty-Dumpty, 79
Hyvrard, Jeanne, 91, 92, 97, 101, 104, 134-135, 153
Irigaray, Luce, 76, 81, 83-84, 85, 88, 152
Isabelle-Marie, 10, 45-57, 79, 84-85, 86, 89
Jahweh, 9, 82, 142
Janeway, Elizabeth, 91, 153
Jeanson, Francis, 32
jungian analysis, 8
Karl, Tatiana, 61-73, 85, 88, 151
king, 2-3, 4, 10, 78, 86
koré, 8
Lacan, Jacques, 135, 154
"Lady of Shalott, The", 136
Laing, R.D., 5, 6, 7, 8, 48-49, 49-50, 51, 52, 55, 71-72, 146, 148, 150
Langlois, Dominique, 33, 34, 36-39, 42 47, 84, 85
language, 4, 73, 77, 78-80, 88-90, 92-93, 94, 99-101, 104-105, 107-111, 113-123, 125, 127-129, 130-131, 134, 137, 140, 142, 150-152
Laurence, 10, 31-44, 45, 56, 57, 79, 84, 89, 134
Le Doeuff, Michèle, 146, 149
Lesbian Body, The, 79, 152
Lia, 17, 18, 20, 21, 22, 26-27, 84, 85
Louise, 45-57, 85
madness, 5, 9, 10, 11, 31, 56, 71, 81, 84, 89, 92-100, 101, 104, 122, 134-135, 140-141, 142
Madness and Civilization, 140-141, 155
Mad Shadows, 10, 45-57, 58, 150
Mandarins, The, 31
Man's World Woman's Place, 91
marriage, 2, 3, 4, 9, 14, 17, 20, 22, 24, 28, 29, 39, 40, 45, 58, 93, 95, 121-123, 125, 140, 142
Mary Magdalene, 80, 83, 115
Mauvaise lecture, Une, 138-140, 154

Millett, Kate, 115
mirror, 4, 5, 10, 11, 37, 39, 46, 49, 74, 76, 81, 90, 95, 102, 111, 132, 135-136, 139, 142, 143, 144
"Mirror Stage, The", 135, 154
Monde, Le, 32
"Mooring Buoy/Moored Body", 101-104
mother, 3, 4, 10, 11, 14, 17, 18, 20, 21, 22, 23, 25, 26, 28, 37, 45, 48, 49, 49-50, 51, 53-54, 63-64, 68, 80, 81, 83, 91, 93, 94-95, 95-96, 99, 100, 102, 138
Mother goddess, the, 8, 91
On the Generation of Animals, 11
Orwell, George, 148
patriarchy, 1, 2, 4, 86, 141
penis envy, 117, 129-131
Persephone, 55, 148
Phaedra, 115
Piatier, Jacqueline, 150
"Pierrette and the Pot of Milk", 99
Pivot, Bernard, 32
prince, 2-3, 6, 9, 10, 11, 13, 14, 15, 29-30, 33, 34, 45, 47, 55, 58, 71, 78, 80, 118, 139, 143, 144
princess, 1, 6, 10, 11, 14, 17, 18, 30, 31, 33, 41, 45, 47, 49, 56, 57, 58, 78, 80, 88, 93, 101, 118, 139-140, 142
Prunes of Cythera, The, 92-101, 110
Pygmalion, 77, 80, 85
queen, 3, 4, 10, 33, 34, 43, 44, 81, 84, 143-144
Rapture of Lol V. Stein, The, 10, 56, 58-74, 88, 150-152
Réalités, 32
Red Riding Hood, 99
Sagan, Francoise, 32
Saint Paul, 26
Salome, 115
Sartre, Jean-Paul, 1
schizophrenic behaviour, 5, 6, 9, 10, 50, 51, 71-72, 89, 140, 142
Second Sex, The, 31-43, 146, 149
sex-roles, 1, 2-3, 9, 11-12, 25-26, 31,

37, 46-47, 51, 54-57, 77, 80, 81, 88, 92-100, 102, 124-126, 136, 144
sexuality, 18, 19, 22, 25, 26, 27, 28, 39-40, 55-56, 59, 61, 67, 77-91, 95, 99, 105-107, 117, 119-120, 129-130, 132, 147, 148
Silent Rooms, The, 10, 13-30, 67, 149
Sleeping Beauty, 7, 10, 58-59, 61, 71, 73, 99, 108, 151
Snow White, 3, 4, 7, 10, 11, 31, 33-34, 58, 84, 99, 102, 143
"Snow White and Rose Red", 109
Solanas, Valerie, 143
Soriano, Marc, 150
Stein, Lol V., 10, 56, 58-74, 79, 85, 86, 88, 89, 150-152
step-mother, 4, 13, 14, 16, 24, 43, 45, 55-56, 57, 80, 81, 102, 119, 137
Stretter, Anne-Marie, 58, 61, 62, 63, 65, 66, 67, 68, 85, 151
Systèmes de politique positive, 11-12
Szasz, Thomas, 146, 148
This sex which is not one, 76, 81-82, 83-84, 85-86, 88
"Three Feathers, The", 2
Through the Looking-Glass, 79, 80, 101, 152
Tom Thumb, 96, 100
Uses of Enchantment, The, 2, 6, 7, 146
Venus de Milo, 114
Verger, Suzy, 149
virgin, 9, 11, 25, 27, 80, 84, 99
Virgin Mary, The, 80, 82, 83, 115
Voltaire, 113, 132
Von Franz, Marie-Louise, 8, 148
witch, 9, 16, 17, 27, 77, 78, 80, 81, 83, 84, 101, 102, 137, 142, 143, 146-147
Wittig, Monique, 79, 91, 92, 104, 111, 113, 114, 134-135, 139, 152, 153
Woman Hating, 148
Women and Madness, 146-147, 148, 150
Woolf, Virginia, 115